Keynote 4

Helen Stephenson

Lewis Lansford

Paul Dummett

and Richard Walker,

Laurie Blass

NATIONAL GEOGRAPHIC LEARNING | CENGAGE Learning

Australia • Brazil • Mexico • Singapore • United Kingdom • United States

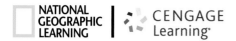

Keynote 4
Helen Stephenson, Lewis Lansford, Paul Dummett, and Richard Walker, Laurie Blass

Publisher: Andrew Robinson

Executive Editor: Sean Bermingham

Senior Development Editor: Derek Mackrell

Associate Development Editors: Yvonne Tan, Melissa Pang

Director of Global Marketing: Ian Martin

Senior Product Marketing Manager: Caitlin Thomas

IP Analyst: Kyle Cooper

IP Project Manager: Carissa Poweleit

Media Researcher: Leila Hishmeh

Senior Director of Production: Michael Burggren

Senior Production Controller: Tan Jin Hock

Manufacturing Planner: Mary Beth Hennebury

Compositor: MPS North America LLC

Cover/Text Design: Brenda Carmichael

Cover Photo: A robot drone hovers above a hand: © Yash Mulgaonkar

For product information and technology assistance, contact us at
Cengage Learning Customer & Sales Support, 1-800-354-9706

For permission to use material from this text or product, submit all requests online at **cengage.com/permissions**
Further permissions questions can be emailed to
permissionrequest@cengage.com

Student Book with My Keynote Online:
ISBN-13: 978-1-337-10413-5

Student Book:
ISBN-13: 978-1-305-96506-5

National Geographic Learning
20 Channel Center Street
Boston, MA 02210
USA

Cengage Learning is a leading provider of customized learning solutions with office locations around the globe, including Singapore, the United Kingdom, Australia, Mexico, Brazil, and Japan. Locate your local office at
international.cengage.com/region

Cengage Learning products are represented in Canada by Nelson Education, Ltd.

Visit National Geographic Learning online at **NGL.cengage.com**
Visit our corporate website at **www.cengage.com**

Printed in the United States of America
Print Number: 01   Print Year: 2016

Contents

Scope and Sequence   6
Welcome to Keynote!   10

1 Embrace Stress!   13
2 Media Influences   25
3 Development   37
   Presentation 1   49
4 Secrets and Lies   51
5 To the Edge   63
6 Money Matters   75
   Presentation 2   87
7 Medical Frontiers   89
8 Life Decisions   101
9 Technology and Innovation   113
   Presentation 3   125
10 Connections   127
11 Life in the Slow Lane   139
12 Make Yourself Heard   151
   Presentation 4   163

   Communication Activities   165
   TED Talk Transcripts   169
   Grammar Summary   183
   Acknowledgements   191
   Credits   192

Featured **TED**TALKS

Kelly McGonigal

1 How to make stress your friend

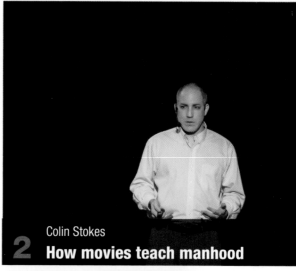

Colin Stokes

2 How movies teach manhood

Hans Rosling

3 Global population growth, box by box

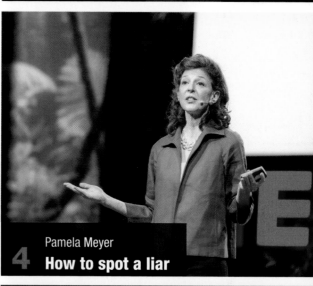

Pamela Meyer

4 How to spot a liar

David Blaine

5 How I held my breath for 17 minutes

Bill and Melinda Gates

6 Why giving away our wealth has been the most satisfying thing we've done

David Sengeh

7 The sore problem of prosthetic limbs

Meg Jay

8 Why 30 is not the new 20

Vijay Kumar

9 Robots that fly ... and cooperate

Julian Treasure

10 Five ways to listen better

Gavin Pretor-Pinney

11 Cloudy with a chance of joy

Margaret Heffernan

12 Dare to disagree

Scope and Sequence

UNIT		VOCABULARY	LISTENING	LANGUAGE FOCUS	SPEAKING
		LESSON A		**LESSON B**	
1 Embrace Stress!		Stress collocations	**Leading a stress-free life** *Dr. Trudi Edginton, psychologist*	**Function** Talking about jobs and stress **Grammar** Gerunds and infinitives	Ways to relax
2 Media Influences		Influences	**Movies and career choices** *Mamta Nagaraja, aerospace engineer*	**Function** Talking about media and inspirations **Grammar** Relative clauses	Ranking movies
3 Development		Goals and ambitions	**International development** *Linda Steinbock, aid worker*	**Function** Talking about change **Grammar** Present perfect and present perfect progressive	Talking about expenses

PRESENTATION 1 Talking about a fictional character who inspires you

UNIT		VOCABULARY	LISTENING	LANGUAGE FOCUS	SPEAKING
4 Secrets and Lies		Collocations with *truth* and *lie*	**Lying in a job interview** *Erin Wong, recruiter*	**Function** Speculating about the truth **Grammar** Modals of deduction and speculation	Speculating about real and fake photographs
5 To the Edge		Describing challenges and successes	**Facing challenges** *Nadia Ruiz, marathon runner*	**Function** Describing accomplishments **Grammar** Past perfect and past perfect progressive	Talking about yesterday's activities
6 Money Matters		Money collocations	**Crowdfunding** *Shree Bose, entrepreneur*	**Function** Using phrasal verbs **Grammar** Phrasal verbs	Planning a budget

PRESENTATION 2 Talking about your most significant achievement

LESSON C	LESSON D		LESSON E	
READING	TED TALK	PRESENTATION SKILLS	COMMUNICATE	WRITING
The stressed-out generation	**HOW TO MAKE STRESS YOUR FRIEND** *Kelly McGonigal*	Involving the audience	Dealing with stress	Writing a letter giving advice
Are superheroes good role models?	**HOW MOVIES TEACH MANHOOD** *Colin Stokes*	Knowing your audience	Assessing movies	Writing a movie review
The economics of happiness	**GLOBAL POPULATION GROWTH, BOX BY BOX** *Hans Rosling*	Using props	The distribution of wealth	Writing about how wealth is distributed in your country
Lies we need to tell	**HOW TO SPOT A LIAR** *Pamela Meyer*	Beginning with a strong statement	The lying game	Expressing an opinion on lying
Magic man	**HOW I HELD MY BREATH FOR 17 MINUTES** *David Blaine*	Explaining technical words	Talking about big achievements	Comparing people's achievements
Giving something back	**WHY GIVING AWAY OUR WEALTH HAS BEEN THE MOST SATISFYING THING WE'VE DONE** *Bill and Melinda Gates*	Being authentic	Convincing people to give to your project or charity	Writing about a charitable project

Scope and Sequence

UNIT		VOCABULARY	LISTENING	LANGUAGE FOCUS	SPEAKING
		LESSON A		LESSON B	
7 Medical Frontiers		The language of discovery	**Drug discovery and development** *Dr. Michael Hanley, biotech executive*	**Function** Making predictions **Grammar** Modals of probability	Talking about future technology
8 Life Decisions		Describing milestones in life	**Comparing generations** *Dr. Laurence Steinberg, psychologist*	**Function** Talking about milestones **Grammar** Future perfect and future perfect progressive	When will you ...?
9 Technology and Innovation		What can robots do?	**Robobees** *Robert Wood, roboticist*	**Function** Talking about conditions **Grammar** First conditional and second conditional	Discussing the impact of driverless cars
PRESENTATION 3 Stating your position on a controversial topic and explaining your reasons					
10 Connections		Collocations with *listen*	**Mediation** *David Walker, mediator*	**Function** Reporting what someone said **Grammar** Reported speech	A survey
11 Life in the Slow Lane		Slowing down	**Living in the present** *Carl Honoré, author*	**Function** Talking about quantity **Grammar** Articles and quantifiers	A multitasking test
12 Make Yourself Heard		Voicing an opinion	**The *Challenger* disaster**	**Function** Talking about the imaginary past **Grammar** Third conditional and mixed conditionals	A moral dilemma
PRESENTATION 4 Talking about a vacation to slow down and enjoy nature					

LESSON C	LESSON D			LESSON E
READING	TED TALK	PRESENTATION SKILLS	COMMUNICATE	WRITING
Just press "print"	**THE SORE PROBLEM OF PROSTHETIC LIMBS** *David Sengeh*	Body movement and gestures	Pitching an invention	Writing a letter to a potential investor
The defining decade	**WHY 30 IS NOT THE NEW 20** *Meg Jay*	Using a case study	Giving advice	Writing an advice column
Drones are here to stay	**ROBOTS THAT FLY ... AND COOPERATE** *Vijay Kumar*	Referring to visuals	Debating	Writing about the applications of drone technology
The lost art of listening?	**FIVE WAYS TO LISTEN BETTER** *Julian Treasure*	Using acronyms to summarize	How good are your listening skills?	Summarizing the results of a survey
Your brain on nature	**CLOUDY WITH A CHANCE OF JOY** *Gavin Pretor-Pinney*	Being enthusiastic	Slow movement organizations	Writing an advertisement for an organization
Whistleblowers	**DARE TO DISAGREE** *Margaret Heffernan*	Using pauses	A company meeting	Writing an email to a company CEO

Welcome to Keynote!

In this book, you will develop your English language skills and explore great ideas with an authentic TED Talk. Each unit topic is based around a TED speaker's main idea.

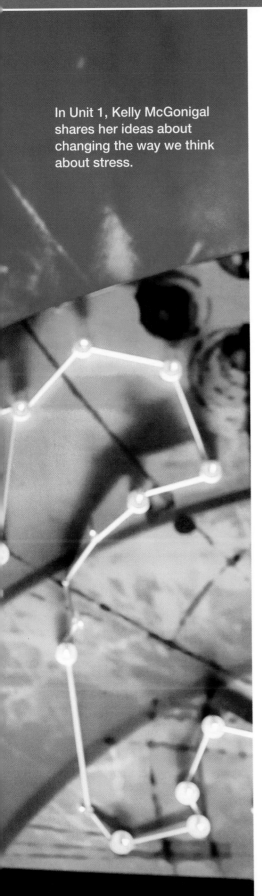

In Unit 1, Kelly McGonigal shares her ideas about changing the way we think about stress.

LISTENING AND SPEAKING

- Practice listening to real people talking about the unit topic. Real-life people featured in this book include a psychologist, an aid worker, and a marathon runner.

- Develop your **speaking confidence** with a model conversation and guided speaking tasks.

See pages 15, 17

VOCABULARY AND GRAMMAR

- In each unit, you'll learn key words, phrases, and grammar structures for talking about the unit topic.

- Build **language and visual literacy skills** with real-life information—In Unit 1, you'll learn about high- and low-stress jobs.

See pages 14, 16

READING

- Develop your **reading and vocabulary skills** with a specially adapted reading passage. In Unit 1, you'll read about why Millennials are facing more stress than previous generations.

- The passage includes several words and phrases that appear later in the TED Talk.

See pages 18–20

VIEWING

- Practice your viewing and **critical thinking** skills as you watch a specially adapted TED Talk.

- Notice how TED speakers use effective language and **communication** skills to present their ideas.

See pages 21–23

COMMUNICATING AND PRESENTING

- Use your **creativity** and **collaboration skills** in a final task that reviews language and ideas from the unit.

See page 24

- Build your **speaking confidence** further in a Presentation task (after every three units).

See page 49

WRITING

- Communicate your own ideas about the unit topic in a controlled writing task.

See page 24

- Develop your **writing and language skills** further in the **Keynote Workbook** and online at **MyKeynoteOnline**.

What is **TED** ?

TED has a simple goal: to spread great ideas. Every year, hundreds of presenters share ideas at TED events around the world. Millions of people watch TED Talks online. The talks inspire many people to change their attitudes and their lives.

SPREADING IDEAS WORLDWIDE

Over **10,000**
TEDx events in
167 countries

Over **2,200**
TEDTALKS recorded

TEDTALKS
translated into
105 languages

Over
1,000,000,000
views of **TED**TALKS at TED.com

1 Embrace Stress!

TED

" I have changed my mind about stress, and today, I want to change yours. "

Kelly McGonigal
Health psychologist, TED speaker

UNIT GOALS

In this unit, you will ...

• talk about dealing with stress.

• read about how stress affects young adults.

• watch a TED Talk about dealing with stress.

WARM UP

▶ **1.1** Watch part of Kelly McGonigal's TED Talk. Answer the questions with a partner.

1 Do you think stress is harmful for your health?

2 What do you think Kelly McGonigal will say to change your mind about stress?

Iranian women practice parkour for stress relief in Tavalod Park, Tehran.

1A Dealing with stress

VOCABULARY Stress collocations

A Read the paragraph below. Then add the **bold** words to the column that describes their meaning.

Many college students **experience** stress. Being away from home for the first time is one major cause; the pressure of exams is also a factor. Since **feeling** stress is common to college life, counselors often recommend that students find ways to **cope with** it. There are many techniques for **reducing** stress. Physical exercise is one. Listening to music is another. In addition, talking to people—especially friends and family back home—can be an excellent way to **relieve** stress. Even though it is a fact of college life, having ways to **handle** stress can help give students a sense of control over their lives.

have stress	manage stress	lower stress

B Work with a partner. Discuss your answers to these questions.

1 What are some other reasons students feel stress?

2 What are some other ways students can cope with stress?

14

LISTENING Leading a stress-free life

> **Showing contrast**
> Contrast words are used to transition from one topic or point to another. Here are some words that signal contrast.
>
> *However, ...* *Nevertheless, ...* *Despite (this), ...*

A ▶ **1.2** Watch psychologist Dr. Trudi Edginton talk about stress. Why is it important to effectively manage stress?

B ▶ **1.3** According to Dr. Edginton, what activities might help us relieve stress? Watch and check (✓) your answers.

☐ painting   ☐ sleeping

☐ meditation   ☐ walking a dog

☐ healthy eating   ☐ volunteer work

C **CRITICAL THINKING**

Reflecting Which of the activities suggested by Dr. Edginton do you think would work best for you? Why? Discuss with a partner.

Dr. Trudi Edginton teaches cognitive neuroscience at the University of Westminster, U.K.

SPEAKING Talking about stress

A ▶ **1.4** Why does Speaker B feel stressed?

A: Hey, what's wrong? You look really stressed!

B: I have an important test tomorrow. I've been studying for it all week, but I feel like I don't remember anything. I just can't seem to focus.

A: Maybe you need to take a break. Whenever I feel stressed, I go for a run or do some yoga. Exercise is a good way to unwind and take your mind off things.

B: I'm too tired to exercise. Besides, I still have a few more chapters to read.

A: Have you been getting enough sleep?

B: Not really. I've only had about four hours of sleep each night this week.

A: No wonder you're so stressed out! I usually get at least seven hours of sleep every night. Why don't you take a quick nap? Then you'll be able to focus better when you start studying again later.

B: Yeah. You're probably right. Thanks.

B Practice the conversation with a partner.

C Work with a partner. What types of activities help you deal with stress? Use the expressions in blue above to help you.

How do you deal with stress?

Whenever I feel stressed, I play video games. What about you?

1B High- and low-stress jobs

LANGUAGE FOCUS Stress and work

A ▶ **1.5** Read about high- and low-stress jobs. What do the most stressful jobs have in common?

HIGH- AND LOW-STRESS JOBS

All jobs can be stressful, but some jobs are much more stressful than others. Below are some high- and low-stress jobs, along with their annual median salaries.

6 MOST STRESSFUL JOBS

 1 Military Personnel $41,998

 4 Newspaper Reporter $36,000

 2 Firefighter $45,250

 5 Taxi Driver $22,440

 3 Commercial Airline Pilot $92,060

 6 Police Officer $55,010

6 LEAST STRESSFUL JOBS

 1 University Professor $62,050

 4 Dietician $53,250

 2 Seamstress / Tailor $25,850

 5 Hair Stylist $22,500

 3 Jeweler $35,170

 6 Librarian $54,500

B ▶ **1.6** Listen to the conversation. Why does Sophie find being a pilot stressful?

C ▶ **1.7** Watch and study the language in the chart.

Talking about jobs and stress		
If you can't imagine having a stressful job, you shouldn't join the military.		
If you like working in a relaxing environment, you should consider becoming a librarian.		
Do you enjoy working outdoors?		
Daniel plans to be a dietician.		
Lara expects to work long hours at her new job.		
Anna hopes to have a career in medicine.		
He	likes / loves	being a teacher.
She	prefers / wants	to work with children.

For more information on **gerunds and infinitives**, see Grammar Summary 1 on page 183.

16

D ▶ **1.6** Listen to the conversation in **B** again. Complete the sentences from the conversation.

1 "I thought you always _____ a pilot."

2 "I didn't _____ such long hours."

3 "I can't _____ papers and _____ people evaluate them."

4 "Good thing I didn't encourage you _____ a professor then!"

E Complete the sentences. Circle the correct words.

1 Jae wants (**to avoid / avoiding**) working in an office, so he plans (**to be / being**) a dietician.

2 Elise considered (**to become / becoming**) an emergency room doctor, but she doesn't enjoy (**to be / being**) under pressure.

3 The university encourages students (**to take / taking**) internships, especially if they plan (**to work / working**) in business.

4 If you are considering (**to have / having**) a career in medicine, expect (**to go / going**) to school for several years.

5 Wei can't imagine (**to run / running**) into a burning building, so he doesn't want (**to be / being**) a firefighter.

F ▶ **1.8** Complete the information using the correct form of the verb in parentheses. Then listen and check your answers.

Many college students ¹_____ (**take**) a semester off from school if they want ²_____ (**get**) some work experience. They often prefer ³_____ (**find**) internships in the types of companies or organizations that they hope ⁴_____ (**work**) for after they finish college. This way, they can learn more about the industry and find out if they'll enjoy ⁵_____ (**work**) in that field in the future. Most students shouldn't expect ⁶_____ (**get**) paid if they find an internship. However, even if an internship is unpaid, students should still consider ⁷_____ (**do**) it. The work experience gained will increase their chances of getting a permanent job in the future, and make the job search process less stressful.

Career counselors help students apply for internships and jobs.

SPEAKING Ways to relax

You are going to ask your classmates how they deal with stress. Turn to page 165.

1C The stressed-out generation

PRE-READING Predicting

Look at the title. Which generation do you think is the most stressed-out?

a Millennials (born roughly between 1981 and 2004)

b Generation X (born roughly between 1965 and 1980)

c Baby Boomers (born roughly between 1946 and 1964)

▶ 1.9

1 Each **generation**—from Baby Boomers to Generation X to Millennials—has its own set of values and characteristics. But one thing common to all generations is that they are suffering
5 from stress. In a recent poll by the American Psychological Association (APA), all age groups now report higher levels of stress than in the past. Baby Boomers (those born roughly between 1946 and 1964, and who are now moving into their retirement
10 years) said that they are stressed about money and health issues. Gen Xers (born roughly between 1965 and 1980) are concerned about work, money, and job stability. However, Millennials (born roughly between 1981 and 2004) are turning out to be
15 the most stressed-out[1] of all the generations. Poll results indicate that stress levels for these younger respondents are significantly above average. So what's worrying the Millennials?

STRESS AND MILLENNIALS

20 Millennials are the first generation to grow up with computers in the home and the classroom. Due to the rise of modern technology and social media, they are constantly bombarded with information. Over time, this information overload can become too much to handle
25 and can result in chronic stress, which in turn can cause serious physical, psychological, and emotional problems. Another contributing factor, according to author Michael D. Hais, is that many Millennials have lived sheltered lives due to overprotective parents.
30 These young adults lack problem-solving skills and may struggle with fear of failure once they leave home. Making matters worse, the 2008 **recession** occurred when many Millennials were graduating from high school or college. The resulting economic
35 slowdown reduced the number of available jobs for graduates. Sure enough, in the APA poll, Millennials said that work, money, relationships, family **responsibilities**, and the economy are the main stressors in their lives.

40 However, the poll results may be a bit misleading as they don't take into account public attitudes toward stress and mental illness. Ronald Kessler of Harvard Medical School, who has studied the prevalence of mental disorders in the
45 U.S., points out that changes in social attitudes have helped reduce the stigma attached to mental

High school students take part in their
end-of-term exam in Fengqiu County, China.

illness over the years. For example, the creation of
health-related television programming and specialty
magazines such as *Psychology Today* have
50 contributed to greater public awareness of mental
health issues. It's possible that younger people
now are more willing to admit to being stressed
than in the past. "There is not a lot of evidence of
true prevalence having gone up," Kessler says. "It
55 looks like younger people are in worse shape, but
unfortunately, we just don't know."

AGE AND OPTIMISM

Despite the high levels of stress reported by
Millennials in the APA poll, there is reason for
60 optimism. Many happiness and well-being surveys
show that happiness generally increases as
people grow older. This seems to imply that the
ability to manage stress effectively comes with

age. As Millennials gain more life experience and
65 develop better problem-solving skills over time,
they should become better at handling stress.
Moreover, with the greater awareness surrounding
mental health issues today, the stigma associated
with seeing a psychiatrist or psychologist has
70 lessened. This means that people are more likely
to seek professional help to reduce their stress
and **anxiety** levels. There is now a wide range of
stress management techniques available including
exercise, meditation, and hypnotherapy. Millennials
75 must develop effective coping strategies to deal
with stress in order to be productive members of
their community. Once they do, they will be able
to look back with satisfaction on the world they
helped create.

[1] **stressed-out:** *adj.* experiencing stress

UNDERSTANDING MAIN IDEAS

Which of the diagrams below best illustrates the results of the APA poll?

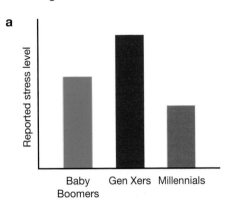

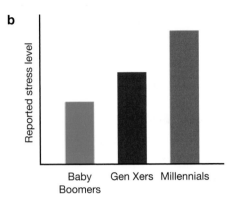

UNDERSTANDING DETAILS

Choose the correct options.

1 Which of the following is true about the results of the APA poll?

   a Stress levels are down for all age groups, but they're down the most for Millennials.

   b Millennials are experiencing more stress than before, but other age groups aren't.

   c All age groups are experiencing more stress than before.

2 Which of these is a cause of worry across all generations?

   a health

   b the weak economy

   c money

3 According to the passage, what is true about young people today compared to the past?

   a They are more likely to become psychiatrists or psychologists.

   b They are more willing to seek professional help to deal with stress.

   c They are more independent and have good problem-solving skills.

4 According to the passage, why might Millennials be right in feeling optimistic about the future?

   a The economy is improving.

   b Technology is helping to reduce stress.

   c Happiness tends to increase with age.

BUILDING VOCABULARY

A Match the words in blue from the passage to their definitions.

1 generation   ○   ○   a period when economic activity is not strong

2 recession   ○   ○   things that a person must do as part of a job, role, or legal obligation

3 responsibilities   ○   ○   a group of people about the same age

4 anxiety   ○   ○   a feeling of worry or nervousness

B **CRITICAL THINKING**

Synthesizing What might Dr. Trudi Edginton (page 15) say about the poll results? What advice might she have for Millennials? Discuss with a partner.

I think Dr. Edginton would say that …

1D How to make stress your friend

TEDTALKS

KELLY McGONIGAL is a psychologist at Stanford University. She is interested in helping people understand and apply the latest scientific findings in psychology, neuroscience, and medicine.

Kelly McGonigal's idea worth spreading is that if we can view stress as our body's natural reaction to a difficult situation, it's better for our relationships, health, and happiness.

PREVIEWING

Read the sentences below and guess if they are correct. Circle **T** for true or **F** for false. Then match each **bold** word to its meaning. You will hear these words in the TED Talk.

1 **Chronic** stress can cause serious health problems.	T	F
2 The way you view stress can **transform** the way your body reacts to it.	T	F
3 Stressful **experiences** can increase your chances of dying by 30 percent.	T	F
4 People who are closer to their loved ones live **relatively** stress-free lives.	T	F

_____   **a** in comparison with

_____   **b** to change significantly

_____   **c** long-lasting

_____   **d** events or occurrences

VIEWING

A ▶ **1.10** Watch Part 1 of the TED Talk. Choose the correct options.

1 What helped McGonigal change her mind about stress?

   a a personal experience

   b the results of a study

2 Who has the lowest risk of death?

   a people who don't experience a lot of stress but who believe that stress is dangerous

   b people who experience a lot of stress but who think that stress isn't harmful

B ▶ **1.11** Watch Part 2 of the TED Talk. Which option best summarizes the Harvard social stress test and its outcome?

    a Participants were told that the symptoms of stress that they experienced during the test were positive. This led to them having relaxed blood vessels.

    b Participants were asked to consciously lower their breathing and heart rate before taking part in the test. This led to them having relaxed blood vessels.

    c Participants were categorized based on how they viewed stress. Those who viewed stress as positive had relaxed blood vessels.

C Label the diagrams below and complete the descriptions using the words from the box.

anxiety	healthy	joy	unhealthy	helpful	disease

1 _____ blood vessel   4 _____ blood vessel

This is a typical stress response when you feel 2 _____ . Over the long term, it can lead to cardiovascular 3 _____ .

This is what happens when people view their stress response as 5 _____ . It looks a lot like what happens in moments of 6 _____ .

D ▶ **1.12** Watch Part 3 of the TED Talk. Check (✓) the statements that Kelly McGonigal would agree with.

    ☐ The harmful effects of stress on your health are inevitable.

    ☐ It's more important to view stress differently than to avoid stress.

    ☐ Forming greater social connections is a good way of dealing with stress.

    ☐ Individuals have the ability to control how stress affects them.

E **CRITICAL THINKING**

Evaluating/Reflecting Discuss these questions with a partner.

1 Check your answers to the Previewing quiz on page 21. Did any of McGonigal's findings surprise you?

2 Have your views about stress changed? How do you think your body will respond to stress in future?

VOCABULARY IN CONTEXT

▶ 1.13 Watch the excerpts from the TED Talk. Choose the correct meaning of the words.

PRESENTATION SKILLS Involving the audience

> Help your audience pay attention by involving them in your presentation. Here are some ways you can do this.
>
> • Ask them questions about themselves.
> • Ask them to make a prediction or guess facts.
> • Describe a situation and ask them to imagine participating in it.
> • Engage them physically by asking them to stand, raise hands, clap, etc.
> • Use a conversational tone rather than a formal "academic" tone.

A ▶ 1.14 Watch part of Kelly McGonigal's TED Talk. Which of the techniques above does she use?

B Work with a partner. What advantages are there to involving the audience in your presentation?

C Work with a group. Brainstorm other ways to involve the audience in a presentation.

1E Managing stress

COMMUNICATE Dealing with stress

A Work in small groups. Read the profiles of four people who are experiencing stress. Suggest possible ways for them to deal with or manage their stress. Use the ideas you have learnt in this unit or your own ideas.

Silvie, 22
- a college student
- is stressed about applying for graduate school
- doesn't cook and eats a lot of junk food
- doesn't have much money saved
- lives near a park

Daisy, 23
- just started her first job
- is stressed because she often doesn't understand what she's supposed to do at work
- lives alone and far away from her family
- enjoys tech gadgets and has a lot of them

Rob, 17
- a high school student
- is stressed about his grades
- lives with his parents but isn't getting along with them right now
- has a few good friends
- loves playing guitar

Theo, 30
- an airline pilot
- is stressed because he works very long hours
- doesn't have a lot of free time to spend with his wife and kids
- likes exercising and being outdoors

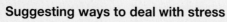

Suggesting ways to deal with stress

She could relieve stress by ...   *It may be good for him to ...*

B Compare your ideas with another group.

WRITING A letter giving advice

Imagine you're a psychologist. Choose one of the people above and write them a letter giving your advice.

> Daisy,
>
> You're experiencing stress because you've just started a new job and it's challenging for you. In addition, you're far away from home. Since you're good with tech gadgets, I would recommend ...

2 Media Influences

" The movies are very, very focused on defeating the villain and getting your reward, and there's not a lot of room for other relationships and other journeys. "

Colin Stokes
Former actor and graphic designer, TED speaker

UNIT GOALS

In this unit, you will ...

- talk about movies and their effect on the audience.
- read about superheroes as role models.
- watch a TED Talk about how movies can provide positive messages for children.

WARM UP

▶ **2.1** Watch part of Colin Stokes's TED Talk. Answer the questions with a partner.

1 What were some of your favorite movies when you were a child? Why did you like them?

2 Do you think movies affect people's attitudes and behavior?

An actor dressed as Spider-Man entertains children at a museum in New York City.

2A At the movies

VOCABULARY Influences

A Complete the sentences using the correct form of the words from the box.

find	have	make

1 Many parents feel that some pop stars don't _____ good **role models** for their children.

2 Some parents want their children to _____ **inspiration** in real people, not fictional characters in movies.

3 _____ a strong **character** means standing up for your beliefs and taking responsibility for your actions.

4 Studies show that even though movies aren't real, they can _____ us feel strong emotions and **influence** our behavior.

5 Christopher Reeve, the actor who played Superman, once said, "What _____ Superman a **hero** is not that he has power, but that he has the wisdom and the maturity to use the power wisely."

6 People with high **ideals** _____ very strong beliefs about what is good and right.

B Cross out the word that is NOT a synonym for each **bold** word.

1 role model	hero	~~actor~~	idol
2 inspiration	encouragement	information	motivation
3 character	personality	body	moral strength
4 influence	determine	affect	help
5 ideals	ethics	morals	suggestions

C Work with a partner. What movies and TV shows had an influence on you as a child? How did they influence you?

LISTENING Movies and career choices

> **Focused listening**
> When you know what the speaker will talk about, you can form ideas. The aim of focused listening isn't to predict what you'll hear, but to help you identify the main points and ideas.

A ▶ **2.2** Watch aerospace engineer Mamta Nagaraja talk about how a movie changed her life. Which movie does she mention?

B ▶ **2.2** Watch again. Check (✓) the statements that Nagaraja would agree with.

☐ Movies can open your imagination to new ideas.

☐ Movies can provide role models.

☐ Movies can influence your career choice.

☐ Movies about space tend to appeal to boys, not girls.

C **CRITICAL THINKING**

Reflecting Have any movies influenced your career aspirations? Discuss with a partner.

Mamta Nagaraja at NASA's Mission Control Center

SPEAKING Talking about movie genres

A ▶ **2.3** Why does Speaker A find action movies predictable?

A: What's your favorite movie genre?

B: I love action movies like *Transformers*. The special effects are great, and they keep me on the edge of my seat. I never get bored watching them.

A: Don't you find them a bit predictable?

B: Not at all. Do you?

A: Yes! The female characters in those movies are usually helpless "damsels in distress" who need to be saved by a man. Most action movies don't have positive role models for girls.

B: Well, what about *The Avengers*? Scarlett Johansson's in it.

A: But there are so many guys in that movie and only one girl. My favorite kind of movies are ones that have strong female lead characters, like *The Help*. That movie had a big influence on me. It's so inspiring.

B Practice the conversation with a partner.

C Work with a partner. Talk about different movie genres and why you like or don't like them. Use the expressions in blue above to help you.

> What kind of movies do you like?

> I love science fiction movies because ...

2B Media and the mind

LANGUAGE FOCUS How the media affects us

A ▶ **2.4** Read about how movies and TV can affect us. Can you think of a movie or TV show that affected you in a similar way?

MEDIA AND THE MIND

People often watch movies to relax. However, movies can affect your mind and your body in ways you may not be able to detect.

NEGATIVE CONTENT:

A U.S. study showed that watching violent movies can lead to an increase in blood pressure and cause hostile behavior in both men and women.

Two psychologists found that elementary school children who watched many hours of violence on TV showed higher levels of aggressive behavior when they became teenagers.

POSITIVE CONTENT:

A study conducted at the University of Pennsylvania showed that watching pro-social TV shows and video clips can lead to positive social interaction and more self-control.

Researchers at the University of Maryland found that laughing while watching a funny film causes your blood vessels to dilate by 22 percent, which helps lower your blood pressure.

B ▶ **2.5** Listen to the conversation. Does Jennifer think it's OK for kids to watch violent movies? Why or why not?

C ▶ **2.6** Watch and study the language in the chart.

Talking about media and inspirations
A role model is someone who provides an example of how to behave.   The movies (that) children watch should be age-appropriate.
Superheroes, who are often based on comic book characters, are not always good role models for children.   The survey, which included people from all over the world, showed that movies can influence behavior.
People participating in the study were all volunteers.   The movie voted most inspirational that year was *The Theory of Everything*.

For more information on **relative clauses**, see Grammar Summary 2 on page 183.

D ▶ **2.5** Listen to the conversation in **B** again. Complete the sentences from the conversation.

1 "I read an article recently about the impact _____ violent movies can have on young children."

2 "It said that kids _____ are exposed to violence in movies and on TV tend to show higher levels of aggressive behavior once they grow up."

3 "But I'd prefer it if my younger brother watches movies like *Finding Dory*, _____ is funny and inspiring."

E Find and correct the mistake in each sentence.

1 Research suggests that watching horror movies releases hormones, which can increase your heart rate.

2 Children that play a lot of violent video games may be more likely to engage in aggressive behavior.

3 One study revealed that movies that make you laugh can lower your blood pressure, that in turn decreases the risk of cardiovascular disease.

4 Parents should be aware of the potential dangers who violent TV shows can have on children.

F ▶ **2.7** Complete the information. Circle the correct words. Then listen and check your answers.

We all know the power ¹(**that / which**) a movie can have on its audience. Movies can inspire, enlighten, or enrage. In 2011, the Academy Award for Best Picture went to *The King's Speech*, a movie about one man's struggle with stuttering—a speech disorder. The movie, ²(**that / which**) helped raise awareness for the disorder, tells the story of King George VI, ³(**that / who**) overcame his stutter to become a great leader of the United Kingdom. Movie characters, ⁴(**which / who**) are often an inspiration for audiences, can help to change people's perceptions of society and the world we live in.

Colin Firth won an Academy Award for Best Actor for his performance in *The King's Speech*.

SPEAKING Ranking movies

A Work in small groups. Below is a list of qualities that are important in a movie. Add three more qualities. Then rank them in order from 1–8 (1 being the most important quality).

___ **a** The main character is inspirational.	___ **b** The movie evokes strong emotions.
___ **c** The movie has a strong social message.	___ **d** The movie's plot makes sense.
___ **e** The movie has actors who I like.	___ **f** _____
___ **g** _____	___ **h** _____

B Pick two of your favorite movies. How do they rate against your criteria above? Tell your group.

2C Are superheroes good role models?

PRE-READING Skimming

Skim the passage. Check (✓) the superheroes who are named as good role models.

☐ Superman   ☐ Iron Man   ☐ Spider-Man   ☐ Daredevil

▶ 2.8

1 Superheroes are everywhere: in comic books, movies, video games, and in posters on buses and trains. But what effect, if any, do superheroes have on our behavior?

5 A research team at Stanford University decided to explore this question by setting up a **virtual** reality experiment. In the study, people were given a mission—to find and rescue a sick child. One group of participants was made to feel as though
10 they could fly like Superman, while another group attempted the same task in a virtual helicopter. After the mission, each participant was interviewed.

During the interviews, the researcher pretended to accidentally knock over a cup filled with pens.
15 People who had just flown like Superman were not only quicker to help, but picked up an average of 15 percent more pens. Every "superhero" picked up at least a few pens, whereas some of the helicopter participants failed to offer any help at
20 all. This suggests that heroic behavior in a virtual environment might **transfer** to helpful behavior in the real world.

Superheroes may have a particularly important influence on children. Children have very limited
25 control over many areas of their lives. Therefore, pretending to be a superhero allows a child to act out and process any anxiety that they have, and thereby resolve or reduce **underlying** fears, claims Dr. Amy Bailey, a clinical psychologist at kidsFIRST
30 Medical Center, Dubai. "Children age three to four years find it difficult to differentiate between reality and fiction and, as such, the trait of superhuman strength is completely believable to them," she says. It "allows them to access some sense of power."

35 Bailey adds, "The risk to superhero play is that sometimes children's behavior can become out of control and escalate into chaotic play as a child becomes submerged[1] in these roles." She advises parents to limit **exposure to** more aggressive
40 shows and to have children focus on "other positive characteristics of their favorite hero, such as their clever thinking and care of others." Concern over the potential effect of aggressive behavior has led to some schools banning superhero play from the
45 classroom altogether.

Other psychologists share this concern. Some point to the evolution of the superhero over time, and are critical of modern renditions.[2] "There is a big difference in the movie superhero of today
50 and the comic book superhero of yesterday," says

Batman impersonator Leonard Robinson visits a sick child at a hospital in West Virginia, U.S.A.

psychologist Sharon Lamb of the University of Massachusetts. "Today's superhero," Lamb says, is "aggressive, sarcastic, and rarely speaks to the virtue of doing good for humanity."

55 Lamb compares the selfish, playboy millionaire Tony Stark (Iron Man) to a superhero of the past, such as Superman. Superman, she points out, had a real job as a newspaper reporter and was **dedicated to** fighting injustice. More recent

60 characters such as Stark "exploit women, flaunt bling,[3] and convey their manhood with high-powered guns."

Jeff Greenberg, a social psychology professor at the University of Arizona, is less critical of modern

65 superheroes. According to him, superheroes give children confidence and can deliver a positive moral message. Many superheroes—such as Spider-Man or Superman—use their powers to protect the weak. And more modern superheroes such

70 as Daredevil, who is blind, and Charles Xavier (Professor X), who is paralyzed,[4] promote diversity and present positive images of disability.

It is becoming clear that superheroes offer us more than just entertainment. "If you design games

75 that are violent, people's aggressive behavior increases," claims Jeremy Bailenson, who led the Stanford University study. But he also believes that video games and other forms of superhero entertainment could be designed to train people to

80 be more empathetic[5] and helpful in the real world— perhaps giving us all the power to be a little more like Superman.

[1] **submerged:** *adj.* deeply involved

[2] **renditions:** *n.* versions or interpretations

[3] **flaunt bling:** *v.* to show off expensive jewelry, clothing, etc.

[4] **paralyzed:** *adj.* unable to move all or part of the body

[5] **empathetic:** *adj.* having the ability to understand someone else's feelings

UNDERSTANDING MAIN IDEAS

Choose the main idea of the passage.

    a Parents should limit children's exposure to violent superhero movies.

    b Superheroes can have a powerful impact on children's behavior.

    c The concept of the superhero has evolved over time.

UNDERSTANDING DETAILS

A Complete the chart showing pros and cons of superheroes.

Pros	Cons
The heroic behavior of superheroes can encourage children to be more ¹_____ in real life.	Imitating superheroes can sometimes lead to violent or ²_____ behavior in children.
Superheroes give children ⁵_____ and send a positive message about protecting ⁶_____ .	Some superhero characters exploit ³_____ and convey a narrow version of ⁴_____ .

B Match the superheroes to the characterizations mentioned in the passage.

    1 Superman ○   ○ He is self-centered and is not a good role model for children.

    2 Iron Man ○   ○ He empowers children and stands for justice, fairness, and decency.

    3 Professor X ○   ○ He shows children that it's OK to be different.

BUILDING VOCABULARY

A Match the words in blue from the passage to their definitions.

    1 virtual ○   ○ having contact with something and being affected by it

    2 transfer ○   ○ existing only on computers or on the Internet

    3 underlying ○   ○ concealed but detectable

    4 exposure to ○   ○ committed to a task or purpose

    5 dedicated to ○   ○ to carry over from one situation to another

B CRITICAL THINKING

Reflecting Discuss these questions with a partner.

    1 Do you agree with the characterizations of the superheroes mentioned in the passage? Why or why not?

        In my opinion, Iron Man is a ... because ...

        I disagree. I think that ...

    2 Can you think of any other examples of superheroes who make good or bad role models?

2D How movies teach manhood

TEDTALKS

COLIN STOKES is a former actor and graphic designer who currently divides his time between parenting and working for Citizen Schools, a nonprofit organization that helps to improve middle schools in low-income communities.

Colin Stokes's idea worth spreading is that movies should feature men who respect women and work with them, rather than men who use violence to rescue female characters.

PREVIEWING

Read the paragraph below. Match each **bold** word to its meaning. You will hear these words in the TED Talk.

As a parent of a girl and a boy, Stokes is interested in how movie characters and **themes** influence his children. In his TED Talk, he **assesses** recent and classic children's films. Several of these movies involve a **quest** where the characters go on a journey to accomplish a goal. However, Stokes is concerned that in most of these movies, both the **heroic** and the **villainous** characters are male. He would like to see more female characters. Stokes believes this is important not only for the girls in the audience, but also for the boys. He suggests that parents **seek out** movies with more female characters, so that both their sons and their daughters can have positive female role models.

1 a search for something, especially over a long time period   _____

2 to look for   _____

3 having the qualities of a bad person   _____

4 evaluates; analyzes   _____

5 the central ideas of an artistic work, such as a movie or a novel   _____

6 having the qualities of a person admired for bravery or great deeds   _____

VIEWING

A ▶ **2.9** Watch Part 1 of the TED Talk. Choose the option that best completes each sentence.

1 When Stokes refers to the "children's-fantasy-spectacular-industrial complex," he's describing an environment inspired by _____ .

   a movies made for children like *The Wizard of Oz*, with simple themes

   b entertainment designed for children that also markets products such as games and toys

   c entertainment that uses sophisticated technology, but is designed for adults

2 Stokes says that the wizard in a modern version of *The Wizard of Oz* might say, "Use your magic slippers to defeat the computer-generated armies of the Wicked Witch," because _____ .

    a movies like *Star Wars* often feature the same magical weapons and enemies as in *The Wizard of Oz*

    b in *The Wizard of Oz*, Dorothy fought computer-generated armies using a pair of magic shoes

    c movies like *Star Wars* often feature a hero who has a magic weapon and fights computer-generated characters

B ▶ **2.10** Watch Part 2 of the TED Talk. Match the movies to what Colin Stokes might say about them.

    1 *Star Wars*   ○   ○ It's unlikely that boys will watch it.

    2 *The Wizard of Oz*   ○   ○ It has strong female characters but is still a war movie.

    3 *Beauty and the Beast*   ○   ○ It can be a great model for both boys and girls.

    4 *The Hunger Games*   ○   ○ It has a lot of violence and only a few female characters.

C Choose the ending Colin Stokes might most agree with.

We need more movies that _____ .

    a focus on relationships and personal journeys

    b present positive messages and role models for girls

    c teach boys how to respect girls and women

D ▶ **2.11** Watch Part 3 of the TED Talk. Discuss these questions with a partner.

    1 What questions does the Bechdel Test ask? Complete the box below.

The Bechdel Test

    1 Are there at least two _____?

    2 Do they talk to _____?

    3 About something other than a _____?

---

    2 What kind of movies does Stokes want for his son? Why?

E CRITICAL THINKING

Applying Work with a partner. Choose three movies and apply the Bechdel Test to each of them. Then discuss the following questions.

    1 Do the movies pass the Bechdel Test?

    2 Why do you think these movies pass or fail the test? Could it be connected to who wrote or directed them? Or when they were made?

        All the movies we chose failed the Bechdel Test.

            It could be because of the movie genre. We only chose romantic comedies, and these kinds of movies are usually ...

VOCABULARY IN CONTEXT

▶ 2.12 Watch the excerpts from the TED Talk. Choose the correct meaning of the words.

PRESENTATION SKILLS Knowing your audience

> Speakers keep their audience in mind when they plan their presentations. When they want to illustrate an idea, they choose examples that they know their audience is familiar with.
>
> When preparing a presentation, think about the following:
> • Where does the audience come from?
> • Are they native speakers of the language you're presenting in?
> • What is their age group?

A ▶ 2.13 Watch part of Colin Stokes's TED Talk. Then read the information below and discuss the questions with a partner.

The first *Star Wars* movie appeared in 1977. People in Stokes's audience are probably familiar with it because they saw either the original movie or one of the many sequels that have appeared since then.

1 Why does Stokes refer to *The Wizard of Oz* and *Star Wars*? What does he assume about the cultural background of his audience?

2 Are you familiar with *The Wizard of Oz* and *Star Wars*? If so, do you think you had a better understanding of the talk? If not, how did this affect your understanding?

B If you were giving a presentation that compared an old movie with a newer one from your country or culture, which movies would you choose? Why? Would these movies work for Stokes's audience? Why or why not?

C Look at the movie poster below. What do you know about this movie? What kind of audience would be familiar with it?

IN THE LAST GREAT WAR ONE MAN DEFIED AN EMPIRE...

"THE BEST KUNG FU MOVIE IN A GENERATION"

NEO

"MARTIAL ARTS CINEMA AT ITS FINEST"

IMPACT

IP MAN

MENTOR OF ICONIC LEGEND BRUCE LEE

35

2E Analyzing movies

COMMUNICATE Assessing movies

A Work in pairs. Create a test—similar to the Bechdel Test—to decide whether a particular movie promotes positive values. First, give your test a name. Then, list some values you think are positive, and think of questions that can help you evaluate a movie in terms of those values.

Test name: _____

Positive values: _____

Test questions

1 _____

2 _____

3 _____

B Get into groups with two other pairs. As a group, choose three movies. Apply each test in your group to the movies chosen. Then compare the results of the tests.

> **Comparing test results**
>
> ... did better on that test.   The ... test is more accurate.

C In your group, vote on the most useful test.

WRITING A movie review

Choose one of the tests above and apply it to a movie or a TV show. Write a review of the movie or TV show based on whether it promotes positive values. Include a brief summary of the movie (or TV show) plot, and describe how the test works.

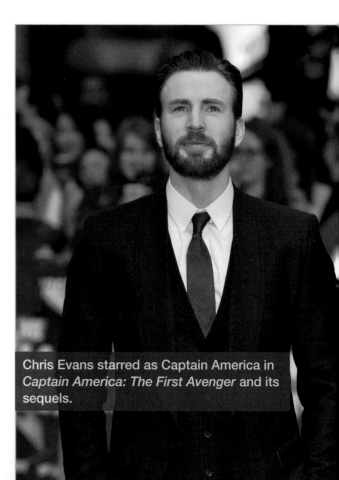

Captain America: The First Avenger tells the story of Steve Rogers, a sickly man from New York who is transformed into super-soldier Captain America. The movie has many interesting themes and—according to the Martinez and Yan Test—it promotes positive values. The first question in the test is "Does the main character achieve an important goal?" In the movie, Captain America's goal is to ...

Chris Evans starred as Captain America in *Captain America: The First Avenger* and its sequels.

3 Development

> And the tragedy is that the two billion … struggling for food and shoes, they are still almost as poor as they were 50 years ago. "

Hans Rosling
Global health expert, TED speaker

UNIT GOALS

In this unit, you will ...

- talk about what people want out of life.
- read about the relationship between wealth and happiness.
- watch a TED Talk about the connection between child survival and population growth.

WARM UP

▶ **3.1** Watch part of Hans Rosling's TED Talk. Answer the questions with a partner.

1 What is the world population now? What do you think it will be by 2050?

2 What are some problems that dramatic population growth can cause?

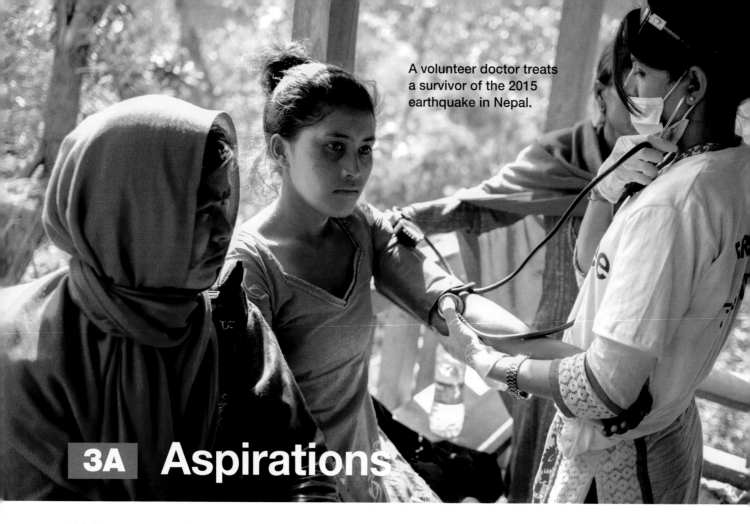

A volunteer doctor treats a survivor of the 2015 earthquake in Nepal.

3A Aspirations

VOCABULARY Goals and ambitions

A Read the paragraph below. Then match each **bold** word to its definition.

What is the average Millennial's greatest **aspiration**? Research suggests that more and more Millennials are interested in pursuing **altruistic** goals, such as helping others. A study conducted by Harris Interactive found that young adults ages 21 to 31 are less focused on financial success than they are on making a difference. Their highest **priorities** seem to be giving back, and working to improve society. This seems to be a worldwide **trend** among young people. As a generation that came of age amidst a global recession, a global war on terrorism, and the Internet revolution, it's not surprising that Millennials tend to see themselves as part of the bigger picture. Many of today's young adults are therefore hoping to go into careers that make an **enduring** impact on others.

1 aspiration ○   ○ the tasks or beliefs that are most important

2 altruistic ○   ○ a general pattern

3 priorities ○   ○ giving without thinking of oneself; charitable

4 trend ○   ○ lasting; permanent

5 enduring ○   ○ a strong desire to achieve something

B Work with a partner. Discuss your answers to these questions.

1 What are your priorities right now?

2 Do you know any famous person who is altruistic?

LISTENING International development

A ▶ **3.2** Watch Linda Steinbock talk about her work at Save the Children. What is the aim of the organization?

B ▶ **3.3** Watch and check (✓) the things Steinbock says influenced her decision to work in international development.

☐ a natural disaster   ☐ volunteer work

☐ a trip to a developing country   ☐ an internship

C CRITICAL THINKING

Reflecting Do you think you could get a job in international development? Why or why not? Discuss with a partner.

Linda Steinbock is passionate about helping children fulfil their potential.

SPEAKING Talking about volunteer work

A ▶ **3.4** Why did Speaker B go to Nepal?

A: Hey, I heard you just got back from Nepal. What were you doing there?

B: I was teaching English to children. I joined an international volunteer program.

A: Really? I've been thinking about volunteering abroad too. How was it?

B: Great! I learned a lot about Nepal and its culture.

A: I've heard that Nepal's one of the poorest countries in the world, and its population has been steadily rising over the past few decades.

B: You're right. I met families who struggle to feed themselves every day. And many Nepalese people can't read or write, especially in the rural areas.

A: Well, hopefully the kids you taught will get good jobs one day. And who knows? They might even become leaders in their community.

B: I hope you're right. It's very rewarding to think that I might have made a difference in their lives. In fact, this experience has made me consider getting a job in international development.

A: That's a great idea! I'm glad you got so much out of the experience.

B Practice the conversation with a partner.

C Work with a partner. Talk about the types of volunteer work you've done or would like to do. Use the expressions in blue above to help you.

Have you ever done any volunteer work?

I'm a volunteer at the local dog shelter. I've learned a lot about ...

3B The next economic giant

LANGUAGE FOCUS Economic trends

A ▶ **3.5** Read about changes in the world's largest economies. Which country has shown the biggest increase in wealth in recent years?

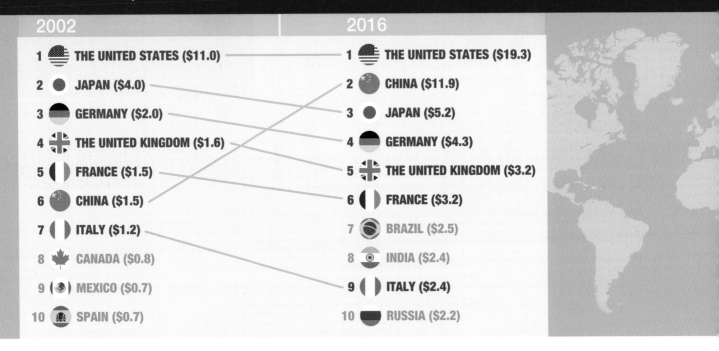

THE NEXT ECONOMIC GIANT

There have been some significant changes to the world's largest economies over the last few years. Below is a comparison in terms of GDP in trillions of U.S. dollars.

2002	2016
1 THE UNITED STATES ($11.0)	1 THE UNITED STATES ($19.3)
2 JAPAN ($4.0)	2 CHINA ($11.9)
3 GERMANY ($2.0)	3 JAPAN ($5.2)
4 THE UNITED KINGDOM ($1.6)	4 GERMANY ($4.3)
5 FRANCE ($1.5)	5 THE UNITED KINGDOM ($3.2)
6 CHINA ($1.5)	6 FRANCE ($3.2)
7 ITALY ($1.2)	7 BRAZIL ($2.5)
8 CANADA ($0.8)	8 INDIA ($2.4)
9 MEXICO ($0.7)	9 ITALY ($2.4)
10 SPAIN ($0.7)	10 RUSSIA ($2.2)

B ▶ **3.6** Listen to the conversation. What are the MINT countries?

C ▶ **3.7** Watch and study the language in the chart.

Talking about change

The world's top ten biggest economies have changed since 2002.
Income inequality in the U.S. has increased significantly since the 1970s.
The world population has jumped to 7 billion.

The economy of China has been growing for a number of years.
Some traditionally strong economies have been shrinking recently.
According to statistics, global poverty rates have been falling steadily for over two and a half decades.

For more information on the **present perfect** and **present perfect progressive**, see Grammar Summary 3 on page 184.

D ▶ **3.6** Listen to the conversation in **B** again. Complete the sentences from the conversation.

1 "Also, all four MINT countries have a growing young population, which means that the labor force in these countries _____."

2 "Unfortunately, poverty and inequality _____ in many emerging countries."

3 "The Indonesian government _____ significant efforts to reduce poverty levels in recent years."

E ▶ **3.8** Complete the information. Circle the correct words. Then listen and check your answers.

Krochet Kids International is a nonprofit organization that teaches crocheting to women living in Uganda, and then helps them sell their crochet products in the U.S. It aims to empower Ugandan women to break out of the poverty cycle. Since 2008, Krochet Kids [1](**has employed** / **has been employing**) 150 women in Uganda. It [2](**has increased** / **has been increasing**) the average worker's personal income by as much as 10 times. Krochet Kids also provides training in money management and business skills. More and more women [3](**used** / **have been using**) this training to set up their own businesses. Due to its success, the organization [4](**has opened** / **has been opening**) another branch in Peru. The women in Krochet Kids Peru [5](**have made** / **have been making**) hats and other items since 2011.

Every woman who works for Krochet Kids is taught how to crochet.

SPEAKING Talking about expenses

Work in pairs. Look at the table below showing trends in U.S. household expenditure. Then discuss the questions below.

	Ten years ago	Today
Clothing	8%	8%
Education	5%	4%
Entertainment	8%	8%
Fast food	1%	3%
Groceries	15%	12%
Health and health products	3%	4%
Housing and utilities	22%	26%
Transportation	14%	18%

1 How have household expenses changed in the past ten years? With your partner, take turns describing the trend in each category.

> There hasn't been any change in the expenditure on clothing. It has remained at ...

> The expenditure on education has decreased from ...

2 Why do you think people are spending more money on fast food and transportation?

3C The economics of happiness

PRE-READING Predicting

Do you think there is a relationship between money and happiness? Discuss with a partner.

▶ 3.9

1   There's little doubt that having enough money is important to your well-being. The ability to afford food, clothing, and shelter is essential to your quality of life. However, well-being is not the
5 same thing as happiness. Well-being is the state of being comfortable or healthy, while happiness is an emotion. So can money also buy happiness? And taking a broader perspective, do countries get happier when they get richer?

10 THE EASTERLIN PARADOX

The idea that richer countries are happier may seem intuitively obvious. However, in 1974, research by economist Richard Easterlin found otherwise. Easterlin discovered that while individuals with higher
15 incomes were more likely to be happy, this did not hold at a national level. In the United States, for example, average income per person rose steadily between 1946 and 1970, but reported happiness levels showed no positive long-term trend; in fact,
20 they **declined** between 1960 and 1970. These differences between nation-level and individual results gave rise to the term "Easterlin **paradox**": the idea that a higher rate of economic growth does not result in higher average long-term happiness.

25   Having access to additional income seems to only provide a temporary **surge** in happiness. Since a certain minimum income is needed for basic necessities, it's possible that the happiness boost from extra cash isn't that great once you rise
30 above the poverty line. This would explain Easterlin's findings in the United States and other developed countries. He argued that life satisfaction does rise with average incomes—but only in the short-term.

RISING INCOME, RISING HAPPINESS?

35 Recent research has challenged the Easterlin paradox, however. In 2013, sociologists Ruut Veenhoven and Floris Vergunst conducted a study using statistics from the World Database of Happiness. Their analysis revealed a positive
40 **correlation** between economic growth and happiness. Another study by the University of Michigan found that there is no maximum wealth **threshold** at which more money ceases to contribute to your happiness: "If there is a satiation[1]
45 point, we are yet to reach it." The study's findings suggested that every extra dollar you earn makes you happier. With so much debate about the relationship between money and happiness, it's

Nyhavn, Copenhagen. Denmark was crowned the world's happiest country in 2016.

clear that happiness itself is a complex concept and
50 depends on many factors.

IT'S ALL RELATIVE

According to psychologists Selin Kesebir and Shigehiro Oishi, happiness also depends on how your income compares to the people around you.
55 They argue that a country's economic growth only makes its citizens happier if wealth is evenly distributed. In emerging countries with high income inequality—where the rich get richer and the poor get poorer—average happiness tends
60 to drop because only relatively few people benefit from the economic prosperity. This suggests that governments should consider implementing policies to ensure a more equal distribution of wealth. The happier people are, the more

65 productive they are likely to become, thus leading to improved economic outcomes at the individual and national levels.

THE KEY TO HAPPINESS

There is continuing debate about the link between
70 wealth and happiness, with arguments both for and against the notion that richer countries are happier. However, it is clear that wealth alone isn't enough to make us happy. The effect of income inequality on happiness shows that happiness is a
75 societal responsibility. We need to remember the positive effects of generosity, altruism, and building social connections. Perhaps our focus should be less on how much money we have, and more on how we use it.

¹**satiation:** *n.* a state of being satisfied and not wanting more

43

UNDERSTANDING MAIN IDEAS

Which sentence best summarizes the main idea of the passage?

a The relationship between happiness and wealth is complex—it involves many societal and economic factors.

b Happiness means different things to different people, and there is no clear link between wealth and happiness.

c People living in rich countries are happier and more productive than those in poor countries.

UNDERSTANDING AN ARGUMENT

Complete the sentences. Circle the correct words.

1 According to the Easterlin paradox, there is (**a** / **no**) positive correlation between a country's economic growth and average long-term happiness.

2 According to Veenhoven and Vergunst, people living in poor countries are (**not** / **equally**) as happy as those in rich countries.

3 According to Kesebir and Oishi, people tend to be happier when there is (**high** / **low**) income inequality.

BUILDING VOCABULARY

A Match the words in blue from the passage to their definitions.

1 declined ○   ○ a sudden increase

2 paradox ○   ○ became smaller, fewer, or less; decreased

3 surge ○   ○ the point at which something begins or changes

4 correlation ○   ○ a puzzling statement that contains two opposing truths

5 threshold ○   ○ a meaningful connection between two or more things

B Complete the sentences using the words in **A**.

1 Income grew in the U.S. during the 1990s, but it _____ in the 2000s.

2 Economists predict that the "Internet of Things" will lead to a _____ in productivity.

3 Researchers have found a direct _____ between happiness and good health.

4 Easterlin's ideas are called a _____ because he found that individual happiness does not correspond with the overall happiness level of a country.

5 Psychologist Daniel Kahneman found that the income _____ for Americans is $75,000 a year. Beyond that, he believes, more money does not make them happier.

C **CRITICAL THINKING**

Reflecting Do you think a person can have too much money? Why or why not? Discuss with a partner.

> I don't think it's possible to have too much money because ...

> I disagree. I think that ...

3D Global population growth, box by box

TEDTALKS

HANS ROSLING is a professor of International Health at the Karolinska Institute in Sweden. He also co-founded *Doctors Without Borders Sweden*. Rosling is known for the creative ways he presents information about global health and economic issues.

Hans Rosling's idea worth spreading is that if we want to manage population growth, we must raise the income of the world's poorest billion people.

PREVIEWING

Complete the sentences with the words from the box. You will hear these words in the TED Talk.

developing world	emerging economies	industrialized world

1 Developed countries that are part of the _____ include Canada, Japan, and Germany. These countries have advanced technology and highly developed economies.

2 Countries such as Brazil and India have _____; they once were part of the developing world but are now increasing in wealth.

3 The _____ is a term that describes the type of economy in countries such as Haiti and Laos. These countries have low levels of technological or economic resources.

VIEWING

A  **3.10** Watch Part 1 of the TED Talk. Complete the diagram below. Think of the props Rosling used to help you.

1960

Developing World

_____ **World**

aspiration: buy a _____

aspiration: buy a _____

B ▶ **3.11** Watch Part 2 of the TED Talk. Complete the diagram below. Think of the props Rosling used to help you.

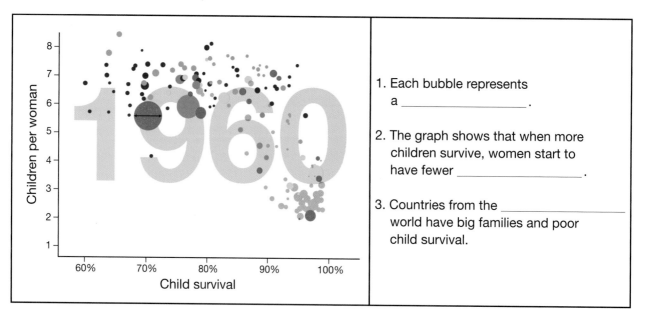

2010

Developing World   _____ Economies   _____ World

aspiration: buy a

_____

aspiration: buy a _____
or a car

aspiration: _____
to holiday destinations

C ▶ **3.12** Watch Part 3 of the TED Talk. Look at the graph below showing the relationship between family size and child survival. Then complete the sentences.

1. Each bubble represents
   a _____ .

2. The graph shows that when more children survive, women start to have fewer _____ .

3. Countries from the _____ world have big families and poor child survival.

D Complete the summary below. Circle the correct words.

As the years pass by, more emerging economies are joining the Western world. This means that the child survival rate in these countries is [1](**improving** / **worsening**) and family size is [2](**increasing** / **decreasing**). However, there is still a wide gap between the richest and the poorest parts of the world. If the Gates Foundation, UNICEF, and other aid organizations invest in poor countries, we can raise child survival rates in those places, [3](**encourage** / **stop**) global population growth, and ensure sustainable development for all.

E CRITICAL THINKING

Inferring Discuss these questions with a partner.

1 Hans Rosling says, "Child survival is the new green." What does he mean by this?

2 Rosling describes himself as a "possibilist." What do you think a "possibilist" is? Give examples to support your answer.

VOCABULARY IN CONTEXT

▶ 3.13 Watch the excerpts from the TED Talk. Choose the correct meaning of the words.

PRESENTATION SKILLS Using props

Props are physical objects that you can use to illustrate your ideas in a presentation. They can also make your presentation more interesting. When you choose a prop, think about the following:

• Is the prop easy for everyone in the audience to see and recognize?

• Is the prop interesting enough to hold the audience's attention?

• Will the prop help your audience remember your main idea, or distract from it?

A ▶ 3.14 Watch part of Hans Rosling's TED Talk. Which of the criteria above do his props meet?

B Work with a partner. Discuss trends in one of the areas in the box by answering the questions below.

communication	food	transportation	money

• What props could you use to show the trends?

• Why would these props work?

• What criteria in the Tip box would the props meet?

3E Rich and poor

COMMUNICATE The distribution of wealth

A Work in pairs. The graph below shows how Americans *think wealth is* distributed in America and how they *think it should be* distributed. How do you think wealth is *actually* distributed in America? Discuss with your partner.

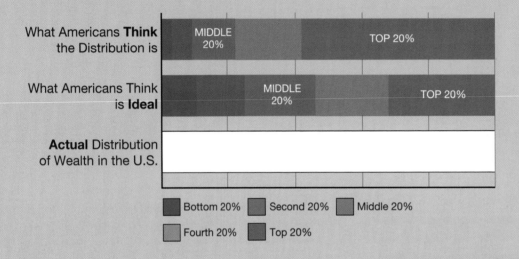

What Americans **Think** the Distribution is — MIDDLE 20% — TOP 20%

What Americans Think is **Ideal** — MIDDLE 20% — TOP 20%

Actual Distribution of Wealth in the U.S.

■ Bottom 20% ■ Second 20% ■ Middle 20%
■ Fourth 20% ■ Top 20%

> **Making predictions about wealth distribution**
> *I think the actual distribution is more equal than ...*
> *I don't think the bottom 20% will own more than ...*

B Draw your prediction in **A** on the graph above. Using the space provided, color in how you think the wealth is *actually* distributed among the five income brackets.

C Turn to page 165 to check your answers. Do you find this information surprising? Discuss with your partner.

WRITING Comparing wealth distribution

Write a paragraph on how you think wealth is distributed in your country or community. Compare it to the actual distribution of wealth in America discussed above. Give examples to support your ideas.

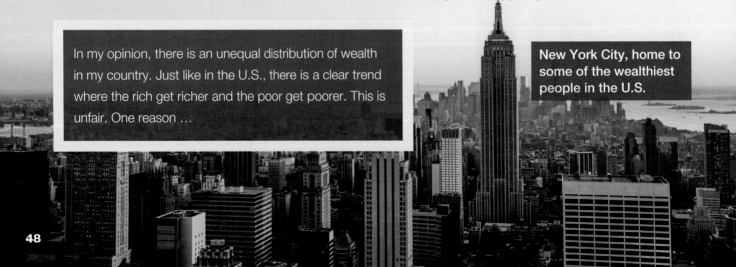

In my opinion, there is an unequal distribution of wealth in my country. Just like in the U.S., there is a clear trend where the rich get richer and the poor get poorer. This is unfair. One reason ...

New York City, home to some of the wealthiest people in the U.S.

Presentation 1

MODEL PRESENTATION

A Complete the transcript of the presentation using the words in the box.

achieve	who	handle	hero
inspiration	quest	has inspired	behaving

Hello, everyone. My name is Justine. Today, I'm going to talk to you about my favorite fictional character, Dorothy Gale. She's the ¹_____ in the book, *The Wonderful Wizard of Oz*. How many of you have seen the movie adaptation, *The Wizard of Oz*? Yeah, most of you have.

Dorothy ²_____ readers since 1900, when the book was first published. Here's why she's my role model. First of all, Dorothy is a team player. She's on a ³_____ to find the Wizard and go home. And she meets other characters ⁴_____ want to travel with her and find the Wizard, too. Dorothy is also a good leader. She's an ⁵_____ to the other characters in the story, and she helps them to ⁶_____ their goals, too. And of course, Dorothy is brave. She's only a young girl, but she's not afraid of the Wizard or the Wicked Witch of the West. For example, she accepts the Wizard's challenge to bring him the Witch's broomstick. She can ⁷_____ difficult situations.

In short, I think we should all consider ⁸_____ a bit more like Dorothy—be brave team players who are willing to lead. Thank you very much.

B ▶ **P.1** Watch the presentation and check your answers.

C ▶ **P.1** Review the list of presentation skills from Units 1–3 below. Which does the speaker use? Check (✓) them as you watch again. Then compare with a partner.

The speaker …
- ☐ asks the audience questions
- ☐ asks the audience to imagine themselves in a particular situation
- ☐ uses examples the audience is familiar with
- ☐ uses props

YOUR TURN

A You are going to plan and give a short presentation about a fictional character who inspires you. The character can be from a book, a movie, or a TV show. Make notes in the chart below.

> Who is the character? Which book/movie/TV show is the character from?
>
> What do you admire about this character?

B Look at the useful phrases in the box below. Think about which ones you will need in your presentation.

> **Useful phrases**
>
> **Beginning:**
> *I'm excited to be here today.*
> *Today, I'm going to tell you about …*
> *I'd like to talk about …*
>
> **Introducing a character:**
> *Here's what we can learn from …*
> *One reason I admire …*
> *What makes … a hero is …*
>
> **Concluding:**
> *In short, …*
> *So, we can see that …*
> *To sum up, …*

C Work with a partner. Take turns giving your presentation using your notes. Use some of the presentation skills from Units 1–3 below. As you listen, check (✓) each skill your partner uses.

> The speaker …
> ☐ asks the audience questions
> ☐ asks the audience to imagine themselves in a particular situation
> ☐ uses examples the audience is familiar with
> ☐ uses props

D Give your partner some feedback on their talk. Include at least two things you liked and one thing that could be improved.

4 Secrets and Lies

"Trained liespotters get to the truth 90 percent of the time. The rest of us, we're only 54 percent accurate."

Pamela Meyer
Professional liespotter, TED speaker

UNIT GOALS

In this unit, you will …

- talk about types of lies.
- read about situations where lying may be good.
- watch a TED Talk about how to spot a liar.

WARM UP

▶ **4.1** Watch part of Pamela Meyer's TED Talk. Answer the questions with a partner.

1 Would you describe yourself as a liar?

2 Do you think it's important to be completely honest in a relationship?

A polygraph—or a lie detector—measures a person's physiological reactions when they respond to questions.

4A Truth and lies

VOCABULARY Collocations with *truth* and *lie*

A Read the sentences below. Check (✓) the correct description.

	Completely untrue	Somewhat true	Completely true
1 Her story had **an element of truth**.		✓	
2 She told **the absolute truth**.			
3 He told **a white lie**.			
4 He told **a total lie**.			
5 He **stretched the truth**.			

B Match each example below to the correct descriptions (**1–5**) in **A**.

a _____ He said he was at the office, but he was actually at home.

b _____ He said, "I like your new hairstyle," because he didn't want her to feel bad.

c _____ He said, "I have two Porsches," but one is his and one is his father's.

d _____ It's true that she lives in New York, but every other part of her story is untrue.

e _____ The CEO began her speech by saying, "I'm the CEO of a company."

C Work with a partner. Discuss your answers to these questions.

1 Have you ever told a white lie to protect a friend's feelings? What happened?

2 Have you ever stretched the truth before? Why?

LISTENING Lying in a job interview

> **Giving examples**
> Here are some commonly used phrases that indicate examples.
>
> *For example, …*   *… such as …*   *… is a case in point.*

A ▶ **4.2** Watch recruiter Erin Wong talk about her experience with job applicants. According to her, why do people tend to lie in job interviews?

B ▶ **4.3** Watch and check (✓) the things Wong says people have lied to her about in job interviews.

Erin Wong is a recruiter for an international IT organization.

- ☐ age
- ☐ reason for leaving a job
- ☐ computer skills
- ☐ previous salary
- ☐ having a certification
- ☐ work experience

C **CRITICAL THINKING**

Reflecting Do you think it's important to be completely honest in a job interview? Discuss with a partner.

SPEAKING Talking about stretching the truth

A ▶ **4.4** Do the speakers think it's sometimes OK to lie in a job interview?

A: Do you think you have to tell the absolute truth in a job interview?

B: Not always. I think sometimes it's OK to stretch the truth.

A: Can you give me an example of what you mean?

B: OK, imagine you want to quit your current job because you have a personality conflict with your boss. And an interviewer asks why you want to leave your current job. What would you say?

A: Hmm. I'm not sure. I wouldn't want to offend my current boss or make anyone feel uncomfortable. What would *you* say?

B: I'd probably say something like, "I'm looking for new challenges."

A: Oh, I think I see what you mean. It's probably OK to bend the truth a bit in that case.

B: Here's another question for you. What would you say if someone asked how long you worked for a certain company?

A: If it's a cold, hard fact, I think you should just tell the truth. Lying about how long you held a job isn't stretching the truth—it's lying.

B Practice the conversation with a partner.

C Work with a partner. Make a list of job interview questions. Which questions could you stretch the truth on? Which ones should you answer with absolute truth? Use the expressions in blue above to help you.

Would you stretch the truth if an interviewer asked you …?

I think it's important to tell the absolute truth here because …

4B Truth, lies, and pictures

LANGUAGE FOCUS Making deductions

A ▶ **4.5** Read the information. Have you ever lied on social media, or do you think your friends have?

LIES PEOPLE TELL ON **SOCIAL MEDIA**
People tell all kinds of lies on social media. Here are some of the most common ones.

 **6%** posted pictures of expensive things that they didn't own — but said they did.

 **10%** lied in order to make themselves appear fashionable or attractive.

 **8%** used some kind of photo app to make their picture look better.

16% of young adults actually believe their own lies after posting them. These are known as "false memories."

 **68%** posted pictures to make their lives look more exciting than they actually are.

B ▶ **4.6** Listen to the conversation. What does Heidi think her friend Sally is lying about? What does Matt think?

C ▶ **4.7** Watch and study the language in the chart.

Speculating about the truth
She might be telling the truth about meeting Will Smith.
He tells so many lies, he may or may not know what the truth is anymore.
The photo of her bungee jumping can't be real—I don't think she's really that adventurous.
He must have used a picture of someone else's car, because he doesn't own a Porsche.
She could have lied to us about her exam results.
He couldn't have been that close to a lion—the picture must be fake.

For more information on **modals of deduction and speculation**, see Grammar Summary 4 on page 184.

D ▶ **4.6** Listen to the conversation in **B** again. Complete the sentences from the conversation.

1 "There's no way Sally got one. It _____ be a picture of someone else's tattoo."

2 "But the tattoo is of a dog's paw print, and I know she loves her dog a lot. It _____ be real."

3 "She _____ have posted it just to see how people would react."

E ▶ **4.8** Complete the information. Circle the correct words. Then listen and check your answers.

Hubert Provand's 1936 photograph of the Brown Lady of Raynham Hall is one of the world's most famous "ghost" photographs, but you ¹ (**couldn't** / **may or may not**) believe the image is real. Some experts have claimed that Provand used trick photography to create the image of the lady. It ² (**couldn't** / **could**) have been faked with a computer, since it was taken before computers even existed. However, Provand ³ (**couldn't** / **could**) have combined two images to create the ghostly photograph. To this day, the photograph ⁴ (**might not** / **can't**) be satisfactorily explained. Even though the image ⁵ (**must** / **might**) not be real, many visitors to England's Raynham Hall still look for the ghost of the Brown Lady.

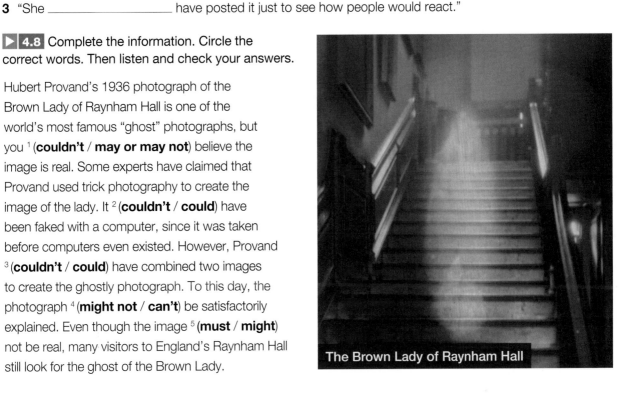
The Brown Lady of Raynham Hall

F Complete the sentences with the words from the box.

must have	may never	couldn't have	might actually

1 We _____ know how Provand created the image.

2 Provand's photograph _____ been digitally altered.

3 The image of the ghost _____ be painted on the picture.

4 Some critics say Provand _____ faked the image by putting grease on the camera lens.

SPEAKING Speculating about real and fake photographs

A Turn to page 166. Look at the two photographs. One of these photographs is real; the other is fake. Speculate about the two photographs, and decide which one you think is real and why.

B Work with a partner. Discuss your answers.

> Photograph A must be real because …

> I'm not too sure about that. The image could have been …

4C Lies we need to tell

PRE-READING Skimming

Skim the passage. Give an example of a pro-social lie that you have told. Share your answer with a partner.

▶ 4.9

1 We often hear "**Honesty** is the best policy," and no one likes to be called a liar. But is **dishonesty** always wrong? Not necessarily, according to some psychologists.

2 According to Oxford University psychologist Robin Dunbar, there are two types of lies: lies that help your relationships and the people around you, and lies that hurt them. Bad lies are lies that harm people; Dunbar calls these antisocial lies. Good lies are lies that make people feel better; Dunbar calls these pro-social lies.

3 How often have you clicked "Like" on Facebook, not because you actually like the picture of your friend's lunch or the cat video your cousin posted, but because you want to show your support? Psychology professor Larry Rosen says that we do this to show our friends that we have good intentions. This white lie is an example of a pro-social lie. According to Rosen, it's similar to saying "Yes" when someone asks, "Do you like my new shoes?" You're lying not to hide a secret or to protect yourself, but to avoid hurting someone's feelings.

4 But when people tell lies on social **networks** to make their own lives seem more exciting, or to make others **jealous**, this is antisocial lying. It doesn't bring friends closer, but instead creates negative feelings.

5 Workplace lies range from small, harmless lies to complete and destructive fabrications.[1] An example of a pro-social workplace lie is complimenting[2] someone on their presentation— even though it was only average—because you know they were nervous beforehand. In this case, your intention is simply to protect your colleague's

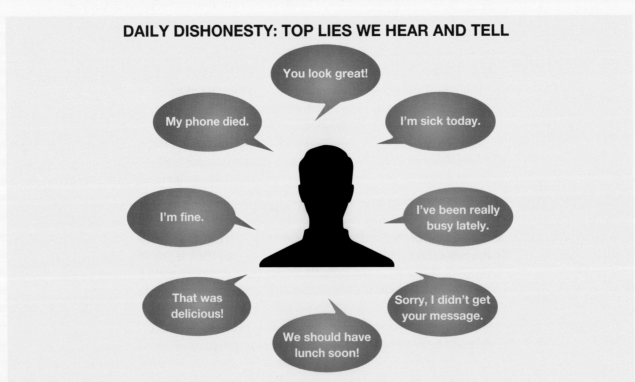

DAILY DISHONESTY: TOP LIES WE HEAR AND TELL

You look great!
My phone died.
I'm sick today.
I'm fine.
I've been really busy lately.
That was delicious!
We should have lunch soon!
Sorry, I didn't get your message.

Koko the gorilla shares a drink with Wilbur Garrett from National Geographic.

feelings. However, people sometimes tell bigger lies at work for the purpose of avoiding blame or to stay on the boss's good side. If your boss asks how a particular project is going and you say it's going well when it isn't, that's an antisocial lie. It's antisocial because your boss is likely to discover the truth, and as a result, will probably stop trusting you.

6   Author and TED speaker Pamela Meyer agrees that not all **deceptions** are harmful. If your partner asks, "Do I look fat in this?" the best answer is probably "No," even if it means stretching the truth. And many experts agree that for married people, keeping some secrets is completely healthy—as long as the secrets don't hurt anyone.

7   Of course, there are some things you should always tell a partner about: the loss of a job or a major health issue, for example. These could affect the future of both people, and living a lie is a bad idea in these cases.

8   Deception is also a significant part of the natural world, so it's little wonder we resort to it almost

reflexively. Koko the gorilla learned to understand 2,000 words in English and to communicate using sign language. Occasionally, she's used this amazing language ability to lie. Human babies sometimes pretend to cry, check to see if anyone is listening, and then start crying again. By the age of five, children learn to say things that are completely untrue, and most nine-year-olds have mastered keeping secrets to protect themselves. As adults, we live in a world where we hear 10 to 200 lies from the people around us every day.

9   Lying can be incredibly harmful to our relationships and to the people around us. But that's only true for antisocial lies. Pro-social lies have the opposite effect—they can actually help us. Through pro-social lying, we can show our online connections that we support them, keep our professional relationships positive, and make our partners and loved ones feel happy and confident.

[1] **fabrications:** *n.* untruthful statements

[2] **complimenting:** *v.* praising or expressing admiration for someone

UNDERSTANDING MAIN IDEAS

A Check (✓) the sentences that are supported by the passage.

☐ Lying always hurts someone in the end: either the liar, or the person being lied to.

☐ Sometimes, making people feel good is more important than telling the absolute truth.

☐ Lying on social media is pro-social, but face-to-face lying isn't.

☐ Some lies can make a marriage stronger.

☐ Babies and children don't lie.

B Match each section below to a suitable heading.

Paragraph 2   ○   ○ Why We Lie

Paragraphs 3–7 ○   ○ Good Lies and Bad Lies

Paragraphs 8–9 ○   ○ Lying Is in Our Nature

UNDERSTANDING DETAILS

Circle **T** for true or **F** for false.

1 We usually tell pro-social lies to protect people's feelings.	**T**	**F**
2 If you make your boss feel better by lying about your progress on a project, it's a pro-social lie.	**T**	**F**
3 Married couples should always tell the truth about big issues, but small lies are probably not harmful.	**T**	**F**
4 Animals are unable to lie.	**T**	**F**
5 Pro-social lying can strengthen our online and offline relationships.	**T**	**F**

BUILDING VOCABULARY

A Complete the sentences using the words from the box.

deceptions	dishonesty	honesty	network	jealousy

1 We typically post pictures online of our best or most exciting moments, which can sometimes lead to feelings of _____ in some people.

2 His many _____ did not become known until years after he had died.

3 The government official's _____ over the financial scandal has led to his dismissal.

4 Through pro-social lying, we can strengthen our _____ of family and friends.

5 Total _____ is probably not important for most relationships. Some lies are helpful.

B **CRITICAL THINKING**

Reflecting Look at the infographic on page 56. Which of these lies have you told and in what situations? Discuss with a partner.

4D How to spot a liar

TEDTALKS

PAMELA MEYER is the CEO of social networking company Simpatico Networks. She has researched lies for many years and has written a bestselling book called *Liespotting*.

Pamela Meyer's idea worth spreading is that by learning to recognize lies through speech and body language, we can help to build a more truthful world.

PREVIEWING

Read the paragraph below. Match each **bold** word to its meaning. You will hear these words in the TED Talk.

> If we're all against dishonesty, Pamela Meyer asks, why is it so **prevalent**? It seems that everyone lies: men and women, **introverts** and **extroverts**, married couples, friends, and strangers. Meyer believes that understanding **body language** is one key to spotting lies. If we know what to look for, we can tell when someone is being **sincere** and when they are **faking** their emotions.

1 honest   _____

2 common; widespread   _____

3 socially confident people   _____

4 people who feel most comfortable alone   _____

5 pretending to feel or have   _____

6 the way we communicate using our face, hands, etc. _____

VIEWING

A Guess the answers to the summary below. Circle the correct words.

Meyer says that [1] (**everyone lies / most people lie**). We lie because we want to
[2] (**protect ourselves / be better people**). We usually lie three times within the first ten minutes of meeting [3] (**a stranger / an old friend**).

B ▶ 4.10 Predict. Complete the sentences below using the words in the parentheses. Then watch Part 1 of the TED Talk, and check your answers to **A** and **B**.

1 We lie more to _____ than we lie to _____ . (**co-workers / strangers**)

2 _____ lie more than _____ . (**extroverts / introverts**)

3 _____ usually lie about themselves, while _____ lie to protect others.
(**men / women**)

4 _____ couples lie to their partners more than _____ couples.
(**married / unmarried**)

C ▶ **4.11** Can you predict a liar's body language? Circle **T** for true or **F** for false. Use a dictionary if necessary. Then watch Part 2 of the TED Talk and check your answers.

		T	F
1	Liars tend to fidget a lot.	**T**	**F**
2	Liars will often freeze their upper body.	**T**	**F**
3	Liars usually avoid eye contact.	**T**	**F**
4	Picture B below shows a genuine smile.	**T**	**F**
5	Liars' actions tend to match their words.	**T**	**F**

D ▶ **4.12** Watch Part 3 of the TED Talk. Use the words in the box to complete the chart.

recommends strict punishment	withdrawn	speaks in a low voice
willing to brainstorm	gives lots of details	enthusiastic
tells their story chronologically	pauses	cooperative

Honest person	Liar

E **CRITICAL THINKING**

Inferring/Evaluating Discuss these questions with a partner.

1 Pamela Meyer says that the behaviors and attitudes in **D** above are "not proof of deception"; they're "red flags." What does she mean by this?

2 Which facts about lying did you find most surprising? Do you think being aware of these facts can make you better at liespotting?

VOCABULARY IN CONTEXT

A ▶ **4.13** Watch the excerpts from the TED Talk. Choose the correct meaning of the words.

B Work with a partner. Complete the sentences with your own ideas.

1 Someone went the extra mile for me when _____ .

2 A politician or other public figure was deceptive when _____ .

PRESENTATION SKILLS Beginning with a strong statement

> The start of a talk is your opportunity to get the audience's attention and hold it. You can do this in a variety of ways.
> • Be surprising: Do or say something your audience won't expect.
> • Be controversial: Say something that some people might not agree with.
> • Be challenging: Say something to make your listeners question themselves or those around them.

A ▶ **4.14** Watch part of Pamela Meyer's TED Talk. Complete the opening sentence of the talk. Which of the techniques from the box above does she use?

"OK, now I don't want to alarm anybody in this room, but it's just come to my attention that _____ ."

B ▶ **4.15** Watch the next part of Meyer's TED Talk. Circle any other sentences that use this technique.

"Also, the person to your left is a liar. Also, the person sitting in your very seats is a liar. We're all liars. What I'm going to do today is I'm going to show you what the research says about why we're all liars …"

only known image

4E Liespotting

COMMUNICATE The lying game

A Work in groups of three or four. You are going to tell your group six facts about yourself. Two of them must be lies. Think about where you were born, experiences you've had, hobbies, skills and abilities, etc.

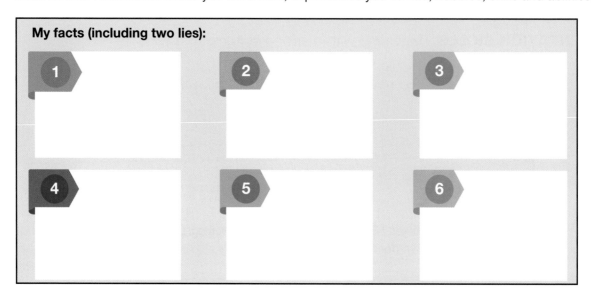

My facts (including two lies):

1

2

3

4

5

6

B Think about how you will try to hide your lies. Consider the following: your eyes, body language, and voice.

C In your group, take turns sharing your six facts. Your group members should try to spot which two statements are lies.

> **Making judgments**
> *That can't be true.* *That sounds like the truth to me.*
> *That's definitely a lie because ...* *I think he/she is telling the truth.*

WRITING Expressing an opinion

Do you think there is ever a good reason for lying? Explain your view and give an example to support your opinion.

Although we often think of lying as a bad thing, there are many times when there may be a good reason for telling a lie. I think that sometimes, it may be better for people to not know the whole truth. For example, ...

Some people give false information about themselves online.

5 To the Edge

"" Magic … is pretty simple. It's training and experimenting, while pushing through the pain to be the best that I can be. ""

David Blaine
Magician, illusionist, TED speaker

UNIT GOALS

In this unit, you will …

- talk about significant challenges and achievements.
- read about David Blaine's endurance challenges.
- watch a TED Talk about achieving the impossible.

WARM UP

▶ **5.1** Watch part of David Blaine's TED Talk. Answer the questions with a partner.

1 What goal did Blaine have as a young man?

2 What goals have you set for yourself—as a child or now?

High-wire artist Nik Wallenda set a world record as the first person to cross Niagara Falls on a tightrope.

5A Challenge and success

VOCABULARY Describing challenges and successes

A Complete the sentences with the words from the box.

| against   break   milestone   overcome   pain   yourself |

1 As soon as you **set a record**, someone else will try to _____ it.

2 To **face a challenge**, you have to _____ your fears and doubts.

3 In many cases, it's necessary to **push** _____ to win.

4 Athletes often **endure** _____ **and suffering** on the way to success.

5 When you **reach a goal** or an important _____ in your life, it's a time for celebration.

6 Sometimes you **compete head-to-head with other people**, and sometimes you **compete** _____ **yourself**.

B Work with a partner. Which of the phrases in **bold** above describe an achievement?

C Work with a partner. Discuss your answers to these questions.

1 Do you know of anyone who has set or broken a record?

2 Can you think of a time in your life when you had to overcome a challenge?

LISTENING Facing challenges

A ▶ **5.2** Watch Nadia Ruiz talk about being a marathon runner. What is her biggest achievement?

   a She has run more than 100 marathons.

   b She broke a national record for the marathon.

B ▶ **5.3** Watch and check (✓) the challenges Ruiz mentions.

   ☐ breaking a speed record

   ☐ competing against yourself

   ☐ following a strict diet

   ☐ pushing through the pain

   ☐ being mentally strong

C **CRITICAL THINKING**

   Analyzing Work with a partner. Brainstorm five personality traits that a marathon runner must have.

Nadia Ruiz has participated in marathons around the world.

SPEAKING Talking about an achievement

A ▶ **5.4** Why does Speaker A congratulate Speaker B?

   A: I heard you won a medal for powerlifting. Congratulations!

   B: Thanks! It was really tough, but I'm glad that all my hard work and training paid off.

   A: How did you train for it?

   B: I practiced weight training every day of the week with my coach. It took time away from my friends and family, and I had to push myself to keep working out. But I'm proud of myself for sticking with it.

   A: It must feel great now that you've reached your goal.

   B: It does. This was definitely one of my biggest achievements. But now I need to focus my energy on next year's competition.

   A: Good luck for next year! I'm sure you'll do well.

B Practice the conversation with a partner.

C Work with a partner. Talk about your biggest achievement in life so far. Use the expressions in blue above to help you.

One of my biggest achievements is winning a ...

How did you prepare for it?

5B Superhumans

LANGUAGE FOCUS Doing the impossible

A ▶ **5.5** Read the information. Which "superhuman" do you think is the most incredible?

DOING THE IMPOSSIBLE
These six ordinary people have superhuman abilities.

28 SECONDS
The time it took **Shakuntala Devi**, from India, to correctly calculate 7,686,369,774,870 × 2,465,099,745,779 — in her head!

-29°C
The temperature when Dutchman **Wim Hof** ran a marathon — without a shirt!

299 KILOGRAMS
The weight of a barrel **Sakinat Khanapiyeva** of Russia moved as a ten-year-old girl — equivalent to the weight of four grown men!

50
The number of marathons American **Dean Karnazes** ran in 50 days, in 50 states of the U.S.!

50

4,700
The number of words **Anne Jones** from England can read in one minute! Most people read 220–300 words per minute.

820 KILOMETERS PER HOUR
The speed of a tennis ball cut in half in mid-air by Japanese sword expert **Isao Machii**!

B ▶ **5.6** Listen. Match each piece of information you hear (**1–6**) to the correct person in the infographic.

Shakuntala Devi _____   Wim Hof _____

Dean Karnazes _____   Anne Jones _____

Isao Machii _____   Sakinat Khanapiyeva _____

C ▶ **5.7** Watch and study the language in the chart.

Describing accomplishments

She had turned 45 before she won her first speed-reading world championship.
He had completed his first marathon before he graduated from high school.
By the age of five, she had already started earning money for her family.
She hadn't known about her superpower before moving the heavy barrel.

When he set his world record, he had been practicing and training for many years.
He had been meditating for several years before he decided to climb Mount Everest wearing nothing but shorts and hiking boots.

For more information on the **past perfect** and **past perfect progressive**, see Grammar Summary 5 on page 185.

D ▶ **5.6** Listen to the information in **B** again. Complete the sentences with the words you hear.

1 "She _____ 40 when she learned to speed read."

2 "He _____ Eastern philosophy for several years when, in the winter of 1979, he decided to jump into some icy water."

3 "He _____ regularly since kindergarten, and completed his first marathon before he graduated from high school."

E Complete the sentences. Circle the correct words.

1 Shakuntala Devi (**was** / **had been**) performing around the world for more than 50 years before she was studied by psychologist Arthur Jensen.

2 Sakinat Khanapiyeva (**lifted** / **had been lifting**) heavy weights for more than 60 years before she finally (**received** / **had received**) the "World's Strongest Granny" award.

3 When Dean Karnazes (**started** / **had started**) the New York Marathon, he (**ran** / **had already run**) more than 2,050 km in the previous 49 days.

4 Anne Jones (**hasn't** / **hadn't**) shown special reading ability before she (**taught** / **had taught**) herself speed reading.

5 Isao Machii (**began** / **had begun**) his training when he was five years old.

F ▶ **5.8** Complete the information using the correct form of the verb in parentheses. Then listen and check your answers.

In the 1970s, Diana Nyad [1]_____ (**set**) many world swimming records—the final one in 1979, when she swam 164 km in the sea from the Bahamas to Florida. She [2]_____ (**complete**) the swim in 27.5 hours. Shortly after that, she retired from competitive swimming. However, in 2010, at the age of 60, Nyad decided to try a new challenge—swimming from Cuba to Florida—a task she [3]_____ (**fail**) to complete 30 years prior. Before her first swim attempt in 2011, Nyad [4]_____ already _____ (**train**) for several months. Swimmers in the Straits of Florida often swim inside a cage to protect themselves from shark attacks, but Nyad [5]_____ (**choose**) not to use one. The challenge wasn't easy; she failed several times. But on her fifth attempt on September 2, 2013, Nyad saw the lights of Key West, Florida on the horizon. At this point, she [6]_____ (**swim**) for 38 hours. She pushed herself through the last 15 hours of her journey and finally achieved success, becoming the first person to swim from Cuba to Florida without the aid of a shark cage.

Diana Nyad is an American long-distance swimmer.

SPEAKING Talking about yesterday's activities

You are going to talk about things you did yesterday. Turn to page 167.

5C Magic man

PRE-READING Scanning

Scan the passage. At what age did David Blaine become a professional magician?

▶ 5.9

1 He's been enclosed in a massive block of ice for three days and three nights, been buried alive for a week, lived in a glass box for 44 days with nothing but water, and spent 5 one week inside a water-filled sphere—all in the name of entertainment. In less than three decades, David Blaine has **transformed** the world of magic. His unique and fascinating career as a magician, illusionist, and **endurance** artist has led critics to 10 compare him with the greatest magician of them all, and Blaine's personal hero—Harry Houdini.

EARLY LIFE

At the age of four, Blaine saw a street magician performing in the New York subway and instantly 15 became fascinated. He started practicing magic with a deck of cards given to him by his grandmother. From an early age, he was also interested in endurance challenges, like holding his breath. In 1987, when Blaine was 14, he heard 20 a news story that really grabbed his attention. It was about a teenager who had fallen through ice and become trapped under a river for 45 minutes. Amazingly, he survived without brain damage.

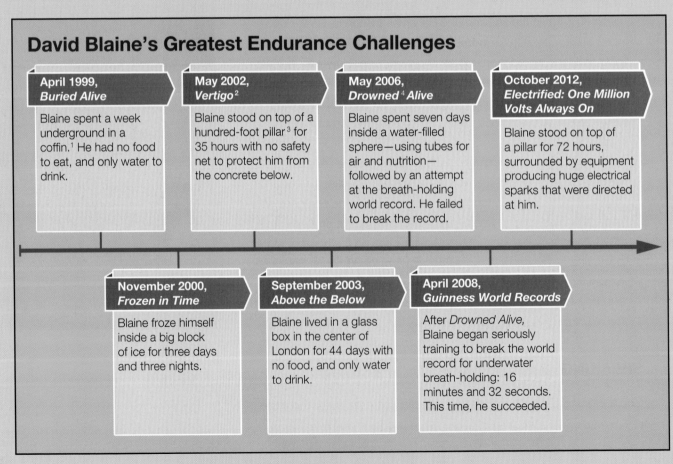

David Blaine's Greatest Endurance Challenges

April 1999, Buried Alive
Blaine spent a week underground in a coffin.[1] He had no food to eat, and only water to drink.

May 2002, Vertigo[2]
Blaine stood on top of a hundred-foot pillar[3] for 35 hours with no safety net to protect him from the concrete below.

May 2006, Drowned[4] Alive
Blaine spent seven days inside a water-filled sphere—using tubes for air and nutrition—followed by an attempt at the breath-holding world record. He failed to break the record.

October 2012, Electrified: One Million Volts Always On
Blaine stood on top of a pillar for 72 hours, surrounded by equipment producing huge electrical sparks that were directed at him.

November 2000, Frozen in Time
Blaine froze himself inside a big block of ice for three days and three nights.

September 2003, Above the Below
Blaine lived in a glass box in the center of London for 44 days with no food, and only water to drink.

April 2008, Guinness World Records
After *Drowned Alive*, Blaine began seriously training to break the world record for underwater breath-holding: 16 minutes and 32 seconds. This time, he succeeded.

David Blaine as seen during
*Electrified: One Million Volts
Always On* in New York City, U.S.A.

At the time, Blaine thought to himself that if the boy
25 could survive without breathing for that long, it must
be possible for other people to do it. And he was
determined to find out how.

THE START OF A CAREER

Twenty years after seeing the street magician in the
30 subway, Blaine became a professional magician
himself. He started out as a street performer and
gained instant popularity due to his exciting tricks
and unique magic style. His success prompted him
to make a tape of his performance, which he sent
35 to a TV network. Soon after, the television network
aired his self-produced special, *David Blaine: Street
Magic*, and its sequel, *David Blaine: Magic Man*.
In these programs, Blaine was shown traveling
across the country and entertaining unsuspecting
40 pedestrians. Unlike other magic shows where
the focus was mainly on the magician, Blaine's
shows focused on the audience's **reactions**. This
forever changed the way magic was portrayed on
television. Blaine had created a new style of magic,
45 and audiences loved it. The *New York Times* said
that Blaine had "taken a craft that's been around for
hundreds of years and done something unique and
fresh with it." *The New Yorker* claimed that he had

"saved magic." Since then, Blaine has produced
50 eight additional primetime specials, including *Real
or Magic*, in which he shocks celebrities in their own
homes.

In 1999, Blaine was ready to face new challenges.
It was time for him to explore his lifelong interest in
55 endurance. In April, he performed the first of a series
of **stunts** that would finally lead to him challenging
a world record. Blaine says, "As a magician, I try to
create images that make people stop and think. I also
try to challenge myself to do things that doctors say
60 are not possible."

WHAT'S NEXT?

Although he teases future plans, Blaine hasn't
revealed his next big project. However, one thing
is certain—Blaine will continue to set high goals
65 for himself and to push himself to do incredible,
impossible things for the **astonishment** of
audiences around the world.

---

[1] **coffin:** *n.* a long box in which a dead body is buried
[2] **vertigo:** *n.* the feeling you get when you look down from a
great height
[3] **pillar:** *n.* a tall stone, wood, or metal object that supports a
building or holds a statue
[4] **drown:** *v.* to die from being underwater and unable to breathe

UNDERSTANDING MAIN IDEAS

Check (✓) the sentences that are supported by the passage.

☐ Blaine's favorite magician is Harry Houdini.

☐ Blaine first became interested in magic when he was a teenager.

☐ Blaine has risked his life for his magic.

☐ Blaine usually competes against other magicians in his endurance challenges.

UNDERSTANDING DETAILS

Choose the correct options.

1 Blaine _____ survived underwater for 45 minutes.

   a once   **b** had a friend who   **c** heard about a boy who

2 Blaine's first TV show was called _____ .

   a *Street Magic*   **b** *Magic Man*   **c** *Real or Magic*

3 Blaine's new style of performing magic for the camera showed _____ .

   a only his hands   **b** Blaine with children   **c** the faces of the audience

4 In his TV special *Vertigo*, Blaine spent 35 hours _____ a pillar.

   a tied to   **b** standing on top of   **c** holding up

BUILDING VOCABULARY

A Complete the sentences using the words from the box.

astonishment	endurance	reaction	transformed	stunt

1 People who run long distances need a lot of _____ .

2 David Blaine's TV specials have completely _____ people's understanding of what magic can do.

3 The crowd gasped in _____ at the magician's skill.

4 Jumping a motorcycle over a moving bus is a very difficult _____ .

5 After the performance, the illusionist received a positive _____ from the audience.

B CRITICAL THINKING

Analyzing Discuss these questions with a partner.

1 David Blaine says, "As a magician, I try to create images that make people stop and think. I also try to challenge myself to do things that doctors say are not possible." What details in the passage support this statement?

2 What other famous magicians do you know of? In what ways are they similar to or different from Blaine?

5D How I held my breath for 17 minutes

TEDTALKS

DAVID BLAINE is a world-famous **magician** and endurance artist who became famous for doing street magic in the late 1990s. He then went on to perform amazing stunts. Blaine has been **obsessed** with both magic and endurance since he was a child—especially the **underwater** challenges of the great magician Harry Houdini.

David Blaine's idea worth spreading is that through training and dedication, we can achieve goals that others might consider **impossible**.

PREVIEWING

Read the paragraphs above. Match each **bold** word to its meaning. You will hear these words in the TED Talk.

1 below the water surface _____

2 a performer who does tricks _____

3 unable to be done _____

4 continually thought about _____

VIEWING

A ▶ **5.10** Watch Part 1 of the TED Talk. Circle **T** for true or **F** for false.

1 As a teenager, Blaine matched Houdini's personal record for underwater breath-holding. **T   F**

2 Static apnea refers to how deep underwater people can go while holding their breath. **T   F**

3 Blaine learned how to remain still and slow his heart rate down underwater. **T   F**

4 Purging releases CO_2 from the body. **T   F**

B ▶ **5.11** Watch Part 2 of the TED Talk. Complete the Venn diagram using the information below.

a has the ideal body type for holding his breath underwater

b is over six feet tall

c had to change his eating habits

d trained for a breath-holding challenge on a TV show

David Blaine   Tom Sietas

71

C Choose the correct options.

1 Why did Blaine change his eating habits?

  a to lose weight   **b** to gain muscle mass   **c** to train his mind

2 Why did Blaine swim with sharks?

  a to be on TV   **b** to get used to the ocean   **c** to learn to relax even in scary situations

3 In what position was Blaine comfortable underwater?

  a floating faceup   **b** floating facedown   **c** floating upright

4 What was Blaine extremely nervous about?

  a being on live TV   **b** wearing a tight suit   **c** keeping his feet strapped in

D ▶ **5.12** Watch Part 3 of the TED Talk. Complete the timeline with the descriptions (**a–f**) of Blaine's challenge.

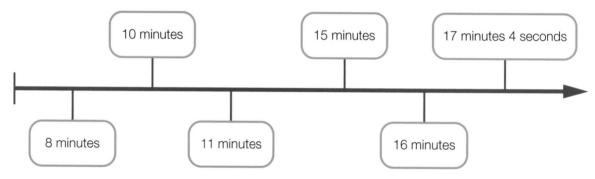

a His legs and lips felt very strange.

b He felt certain he wouldn't be able to complete the challenge.

c He pulled his feet out of the straps.

d He started to get strange feelings in his fingers and toes.

e He set a new world record.

f He experienced an irregular heartbeat.

E CRITICAL THINKING

Reflecting Look back at David Blaine's endurance challenges on page 68. Given how dangerous they are, should we really be watching them? Do you think there is a point where entertainment like this becomes irresponsible? Discuss with a partner.

VOCABULARY IN CONTEXT

A ▶ **5.13** Watch the excerpts from the TED Talk. Choose the correct meaning of the words.

B Work in pairs. Complete the sentences with your own ideas.

1 Foods that have high nutritional value, such as _____, are good for our health.

2 One of the primetime shows that people are watching now is _____.

3 Once, I felt lightheaded when _____.

PRESENTATION SKILLS Explaining technical words

Sometimes speakers use technical terms and then immediately define them. Giving definitions can help your audience understand difficult words.

• Include technical terms only when they're essential to your message. Learn to distinguish between essential and non-essential terms.

• Explain technical terms as soon as you use them for the first time.

A ▶ **5.14** Watch part of David Blaine's TED Talk. Match each technical term to the definition he gives.

1 static apnea ○   ○ blowing in and out quickly

2 purging, hyperventilating ○   ○ when the blood rushes away from your arms and legs

3 buoyant ○   ○ holding your breath without moving

4 blood shunting ○   ○ when your heartbeat changes suddenly

5 ischemia ○   ○ floating

B You are going to talk briefly on a topic of your choice. It could be a sport, a hobby, or something you learned in school. Make brief notes on what you want to say, and choose two or three technical terms that are essential to your message.

C Work with a partner. Take turns giving your presentations, and explain the technical terms you chose in **B**.

David Blaine interacts with a passerby during *Drowned Alive*.

5E Explaining achievements

COMMUNICATE Talking about big achievements

A Think of someone who has achieved something extraordinary in sports, science, the arts, or any other area. Do research and make notes. Consider the following questions.

What did the person achieve? _____

When did they achieve this? _____

How did they train or prepare for it? _____

B Work in groups of three or four. Talk about the person you researched.

> **Describing achievements**
>
> *He/She made history by ...*   *He/She made a significant contribution to ...*
> *He/She succeeded in ...*   *He/She set a record for being ...*

> In 1975, Junko Tabei became the first woman to reach the summit of Mount Everest. Her climbing team was made up of 15 women, including teachers and a computer programmer. To prepare for her climb, Tabei ...

C Of the people you talked about in **B**, which achievement do you think was the most difficult? Which achievement would you most like to emulate? Discuss with your group members.

WRITING Making a comparison

Choose one of the people you discussed above, and compare and contrast their achievements with David Blaine's. Include details about how they prepared to reach their goals.

> Junko Tabei was a mountain climber, while David Blaine is a magician and endurance artist. These are two very different activities. However, both of them had a strong desire to achieve difficult goals and worked very hard to reach them. Tabei trained on higher and higher mountains, and ...

Junko Tabei was the first woman to reach the summit of Mount Everest.

6 Money Matters

"You can't take it with you."

Bill and Melinda Gates
Corporate leaders, philanthropists, TED speakers

UNIT GOALS

In this unit, you will …

- talk about crowdfunding and giving to charity.
- read about how wealthy people have used their money.
- watch a TED Talk about using wealth responsibly.

WARM UP

▶ 6.1 Watch part of Bill and Melinda Gates's TED Talk. Answer the questions with a partner.

1 What does Bill Gates think the wealthiest people should do with their money?

2 What is Melinda Gates trying to change in the U.S.?

Bank officers count money at a shrine in Kyoto, Japan.

6A Money

VOCABULARY Money collocations

A Complete the collocations. Add the words in the box to the correct column.

| interest | an investment | services | an income | to charity | a difference |

make	earn	donate
a contribution	a living	money

B Complete the sentences using the correct form of the words in the chart above.

1 In 2016, Warren Buffett _____ nearly $2.9 billion to the Bill & Melinda Gates Foundation and other charities.

2 It can be difficult to earn _____ as a musician.

3 Many companies make _____ to their employees' pension plan.

4 My mother often works overtime to earn extra _____ .

5 My money earns a little _____ from the bank.

C Work with a partner. Discuss your answers to these questions.

1 What are some things you can invest your money in?

2 Would you rather donate time or money to a charity? Why?

LISTENING Crowdfunding

> **Listening for gist**
> The big picture can be just as important as the specifics. When finding the gist of a talk, focus on the main ideas you understand and try to work out the connections between them. Don't worry if you don't understand every phrase or sentence.

A ▶ **6.2** Watch entrepreneur Shree Bose talk about launching a crowdfunding campaign. How does it work?

    a by asking a few people to donate big sums of money

    b by asking many people to donate a small amount of money

B ▶ **6.2** Watch again. Check (✓) the benefits of crowdfunding Bose mentions.

    ☐ It can help demonstrate the demand for a new product.

    ☐ It's a great way to reach people from all over the world.

    ☐ It minimizes the financial risk to investors.

    ☐ It can help to create a loyal customer base.

C **CRITICAL THINKING**

Evaluating **Can you think of any downsides to crowdfunding? Discuss with a partner.**

Shree Bose started her company Piper through crowdfunding.

SPEAKING Talking about making a contribution

A ▶ **6.3** What is Speaker B's opinion about crowdfunding?

    A: Would you make a crowdfunding contribution to Piper?

    B: I'm not sure. It sounds like a good idea, but I'd rather invest in it after I've seen and used the product.

    A: I see your point. But I think it's a great way to support a company—investing some money in it and helping it to develop its idea.

    B: I don't know. Shouldn't a business just get a bank loan or get investors to help them?

    A: Maybe. But with crowdfunding, you build a relationship with the company. You aren't just giving them your money; you're paying for a product you believe in, and you usually get rewards in exchange.

    B: OK, I guess some people enjoy feeling like they're part of the process. But personally, I'd prefer to donate money to a charity—to help wildlife or something like that, or to help people.

B Practice the conversation with a partner.

C Work with a partner. Look up the Kickstarter website and select a project. Would you donate money to support it? What would you want in return? Use the expressions in blue above to help you.

> I'd support ... and invest money in it. It sounds like an interesting idea.

> I'd only invest in it if I get ... in return.

6B What we're saving for

LANGUAGE FOCUS Talking about saving habits

A ▶ **6.4** Read about what Australians save money for. Do you save money regularly? What are you saving for?

WHAT AUSTRALIANS **SAVE MONEY FOR**

EVERYONE SAVES MONEY FOR DIFFERENT REASONS. HERE'S WHAT MOST AUSTRALIANS SAVE FOR.

48% A HOME	**47%** A VACATION	**33%** AN EMERGENCY FUND	**13%** A CAR
10% EDUCATION	**8%** FURNITURE/APPLIANCES	**5%** A WEDDING	**4%** A NEW COMPUTER/TECHNOLOGY

B ▶ **6.5** Listen. What is each person saving for? Write the reasons from the infographic.

1 _____   4 _____

2 _____   5 _____

3 _____   6 _____

C ▶ **6.6** Watch and study the language in the chart.

> **Using phrasal verbs**
>
> **Separable**
> We're putting aside some funds for our vacation.
> We're putting a few thousand dollars aside for our house renovation.
> We brought up our children to be polite.
> We brought our children up well.
>
> **Not separable**
> The coach really believes in the team.
> I need to save money in case I lose my job or my car breaks down.
> Eric does without a car because he wants to protect the environment.

For more information on **phrasal verbs**, see Grammar Summary 6 on page 185.

D ▶ **6.5** Listen to the information in **B** again. Complete the sentences with the words you hear.

1 "We're _____ about two hundred dollars a month right now."

2 "We're _____ two kids, and we just have a small flat that we're renting."

3 "I haven't _____ what I want to study, but I definitely want to go to university."

E Read the paragraph below. Match each **bold** verb to the phrasal verb that has the same meaning.

Household savings rates can be very different across different countries. *Global Finance* magazine **researched** how much families around the world save, and **discovered** that while richer countries generally have higher savings rates, not all wealthy countries save a lot. In 2015, the best savers in the world were the Swiss, who **saved** over 17 percent of their household income. However, Denmark's household savings in 2015 was very low, at about -4 percent. This could be due to the Danes' confidence in the economy, Denmark's well-developed social security system, and other factors that **create** more equal distribution of incomes in the country.

1 researched ○		○ found out
2 discovered ○		○ result in
3 saved ○		○ looked into
4 create ○		○ put aside

Household savings rates are often an indicator of how well a country's economy is doing.

F Put the words in the correct order to make sentences or questions.

1 off / We / loan / our / paid

_____ .

2 think / Let's / options / our / over

_____ .

3 payments / Can / the / we / out / spread

_____ ?

4 set / you / Do / much / aside / money

_____ ?

5 give / up / going to / I'm / restaurants / expensive

_____ .

6 is / Bill Gates / away / giving / money / his / of / most

_____ .

SPEAKING Planning a budget

A Work with a partner and plan a budget together. Look at the infographic on page 78. Which of these things would you save for? How much of your budget would you set aside?

I'd set aside ... for a vacation to Bali.

I don't think that's enough. We may have to give up ... to save more money.

B Share your budget with another pair. Discuss the similarities and differences.

6C Giving something back

PRE-READING Scanning

Scan the passage. Who's the world's biggest charity donor?

▶ 6.7

1 Whether they're donating to disaster relief funds, education, or healthcare, these **celebrity** couples have made a habit of giving their wealth away, and are inspiring many
5 others to do the same.

SHAKIRA AND GERARD PIQUÉ

She's a Colombian pop star who has sold over 70 million albums worldwide. He's a Spanish soccer star with a World Cup title to his name. They met
10 in 2010 when Piqué appeared in Shakira's music video for "Waka Waka (This Time for Africa)"—the official song of the 2010 FIFA World Cup—and have been together ever since. After three years together, the couple welcomed their first son, Milan, followed
15 by their second little boy, Sasha, in 2015.

The birth of both children prompted the couple to give back. They set up a World Baby Shower in the lead-up to each birth, and asked fans to send gifts to other babies around the world who were
20 in need of help. Both of these Baby Showers were huge successes, raising more than $200,000 for food, medicines, and blankets. Shakira said she hoped her two boys would appreciate what she'd done and be inspired themselves. "My hope is that
25 by the time my sons are adults, they can look back and see how even small efforts can have a big impact when multiplied," she wrote in her blog.

Shakira is also a Goodwill Ambassador for UNICEF (United Nations Children's Emergency Fund).
30 In fact, she has long been involved in promoting children's rights. When she was only 18, Shakira set up the Barefoot **Foundation**. This organization educates and feeds more than 6,000 children in Colombia and other countries. Her charities have
35 received donations as high as $200 million from Carlos Slim, Mexico's richest man, and Howard Buffett, son of American billionaire Warren Buffett.

BILL AND MELINDA GATES

With a net worth of $81 billion, they're the wealthiest
40 couple on the planet. And according to *Forbes* magazine, they're the world's most generous as well. Bill Gates amassed billions of dollars after Microsoft **took off** in 1980. Along with his wife Melinda—who was once a Microsoft employee
45 herself—Bill now works full-time as co-chair of the

The world's biggest charity donors (2015)	
$28 billion	**Bill Gates** has donated $28 billion of his fortune to his own charity, the Bill & Melinda Gates Foundation.
$21.5 billion	**Warren Buffett**, one of the richest men in the world, has pledged to donate the bulk of his fortune to the Bill & Melinda Gates Foundation and four other charities.
£5.1 billion	Businessman and investor **George Soros** has donated his wealth to educational and healthcare institutes across the world.
$6.8 billion	**Gordon Moore**, technology pioneer and Intel founder, has donated $6.8 billion to the charity he founded with his wife—the Gordon and Betty Moore Foundation.
$498 million	Facebook CEO **Mark Zuckerberg** has donated to various causes such as public schools and the Silicon Valley Community Foundation.

Shakira meets with local children on a visit to Bangladesh.

Bill & Melinda Gates Foundation. The foundation was set up in 1997 and works to improve healthcare, reduce **poverty**, and increase access to education and information technology worldwide. One of the
50 foundation's primary goals is to eradicate[1] polio worldwide by 2018. The couple practice what they preach,[2] and have traveled to hospitals and remote villages all over the world to help those in need.

In 2006, Warren Buffett joined the cause
55 when he **pledged** to give about $30 billion to the Gates Foundation—the largest donation to charity in history. And on December 9, 2010, Gates, Buffett, and Mark Zuckerberg—CEO of Facebook—signed the "Gates-Buffett Giving
60 Pledge": a promise to donate half of their wealth to charity, and also to try to get other wealthy people to do the same.

[1] **eradicate:** *v.* to remove completely
[2] **to practice what you preach:** *v.* to do what you advise other people to do

UNDERSTANDING MAIN IDEAS

Complete the Venn diagram using the information below.

a have ties to the Buffett family

b have a foundation named after themselves

c were inspired to give back after becoming parents

d have donated money for education

e are the wealthiest couple in the world

f use their fame from sports and entertainment to raise awareness of children's issues

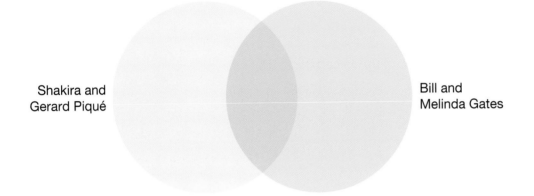

Shakira and Gerard Piqué

Bill and Melinda Gates

UNDERSTANDING DETAILS

Match each organization or initiative to its purpose.

1 World Baby Shower ○   ○ to provide Colombian children with access to education

2 UNICEF ○   ○ to eradicate poverty and polio globally

3 Barefoot Foundation ○   ○ to give newborns a healthy start in life

4 Bill & Melinda Gates Foundation ○   ○ to encourage wealthy individuals to donate to charity

5 Gates-Buffett Giving Pledge ○   ○ to respond to emergencies in developing countries by providing aid for children

BUILDING VOCABULARY

A Complete the sentences with the words from the box.

foundation	pledge	poverty	celebrities	take off

1 Would you _____ to give part of your wealth to help poor people?

2 They established a _____ because they wanted to give away their money.

3 It often benefits charities to have _____ help spread their message.

4 George Soros's wealth is even more amazing given that he grew up in _____.

5 He worked hard for many years before his business really began to _____.

B CRITICAL THINKING

Reflecting Would you be more likely to donate to a charity if it is supported by a celebrity? Why or why not? Discuss with a partner.

6D Why giving away our wealth has been the most satisfying thing we've done

1**TED**TALKS

BILL AND MELINDA GATES are the world's wealthiest couple and also two of its most generous philanthropists.

Bill and Melinda Gates's idea worth spreading is that entrepreneurs who have succeeded in business can use their wealth and knowledge to help deal with the world's biggest problems.

PREVIEWING

Read the paragraph below. Circle the correct meaning of each **bold** word. You will hear these words in the TED Talk.

Many of us dream of becoming wealthy, but the most **satisfying** thing Bill and Melinda Gates have done is to give their money away. Their **philosophy** for raising their children has been to teach them that **philanthropy** is more important than money. The Gates family believes that being wealthy is a great **responsibility**. Their mission is not only to give their own money away, but to encourage other wealthy people to do the same to help make the world a more **just** place.

1 Something that is **satisfying** gives you feelings of (**calmness / pleasure**).

2 The **philosophy** behind something refers to the (**ideas and attitude / uncertainty**) behind it.

3 **Philanthropy** refers to the effort you put in to (**distract / help**) other people.

4 If you have a great **responsibility**, you have a lot of (**power / common sense**).

5 A world that is more **just** is more (**fair / unfair**).

VIEWING

A ▶ 6.8 Watch Part 1 of the TED Talk. Check (✓) the ideas Bill and Melinda Gates would agree with.

☐ Giving children a good education is more important than giving them money.

☐ Children should be allowed to choose their own direction in life.

☐ Wealthy people should give something back to the world.

☐ Wealthy parents should limit their children's exposure to the outside world for safety reasons.

☐ Wealthy people should only invest money in profitable businesses.

83

B ▶ **6.9** Watch Part 2 of the TED Talk. Choose the correct options.

1 How much of their wealth have the Gates pledged to give away?

   a $95 billion   **b** 95%

2 The Gates and Warren Buffett have been trying to persuade other billionaires to donate _____ of their assets for philanthropy.

   a a quarter   **b** more than half

3 How many people have taken the Giving Pledge?

   a fewer than 100 people   **b** over 100 people

4 The participants of the Giving Pledge meet every year to talk about _____.

   a different ways of doing good   **b** how government policies can be improved

5 According to Bill Gates, one of the best things about philanthropy is its _____.

   a diversity   **b** history

6 According to Melinda Gates, what must philanthropists have to inspire change?

   a creativity and drive   **b** good speaking skills

C ▶ **6.10** Guess the answers to complete the sentences below. Circle the correct words. Then watch Part 3 of the TED Talk and check your answers.

1 According to Bill Gates, (**the U.S.** / **Canada**) has the strongest tradition of philanthropy in the world.

2 Bill Gates is (**doubtful** / **optimistic**) that philanthropy can help solve problems governments aren't good at working on.

3 The interviewer, Chris Anderson, believes that the world has a terrible (**inequality** / **debt**) problem.

4 Melinda Gates believes that the best way to address the (**inequality** / **debt**) problem is to change the (**financial** / **education**) system.

D ▶ **6.10** Watch Part 3 of the TED Talk again. Complete the sentences below summarizing Bill Gates's pitch to other billionaires.

1 It's the most fulfilling thing he's _____.

2 You can't _____ with you.

3 It's _____ for your kids.

E CRITICAL THINKING

Inferring/Reflecting Discuss these questions with a partner.

1 Look again at Bill Gates's pitch in **D**. How does he persuade other billionaires to donate their wealth?

> First, he explains that it gives him a great sense of satisfaction.

> Next, he points out that ...

2 Imagine you have $28 billion. What percentage of your wealth would you give away, and to what cause(s)?

VOCABULARY IN CONTEXT

A ▶ **6.11** Watch the excerpts from the TED Talk. Choose the correct meaning of the words.

B Work with a partner. Complete the sentences with your own ideas.

1 It's important to strike a balance between _____ and _____ .

2 I would like to be wealthy so I could shower money on _____ .

3 We may not be able to end hunger or poverty worldwide by _____ , but we can at least make a dent in the problem.

PRESENTATION SKILLS Being authentic

The way you deliver your talk should reflect your personality. Whether you're naturally funny, serious, shy, or self-confident, you should be yourself. It's important to:

• relax so that you move and gesture naturally;

• wear clothes you feel comfortable in;

• use words and expressions you normally use; and

• not worry about being perfect. Audiences respond to speakers who are natural.

A ▶ **6.12** Watch part of Bill and Melinda Gates's TED Talk. How does Bill use the techniques from the box above?

B Work with a partner. Discuss your answers to these questions.

1 Is Bill Gates comfortable and relaxed? How can you tell?

2 What do you think your personal style is? Are you funny or serious, or something else?

3 If you had to give a TED Talk, what clothes would you choose to wear? Why?

4 Would you wear something different if you were just giving a presentation in class? Why or why not?

Bill Gates with One.org charity volunteers in Berlin, Germany

6E Creating a charity

COMMUNICATE Convincing people to give to your project or charity

A Make some notes about a project you would like to raise money for. It could be a charitable project to make the world a better place, a business you want to start, or something just for yourself.

What I want to do	Why I want to do it	How much money I'll need

B Work in groups of three or four. Explain your project to your group members.

> I'd like to raise money to pay for acting lessons for myself. I think I could be a great actor. I'll probably need about $20,000.

> I'd like to help reduce pollution, so I want to raise money to buy electric buses for my city. I think I'll need about a million dollars.

C In your group, discuss these questions: Who might give money to fund each project? What could each project possibly give back to the world? Which project do you think is the most likely to be funded?

D After your group has chosen the project most likely to be funded, take turns explaining it and presenting your funding ideas to the class. Then vote for the best project or charity.

> **Presenting a proposal**
> *The ultimate goal of our project is ...*   *We estimate that it will cost ...*
> *This project will help ...*   *We intend to raise ... dollars by ...*

WRITING Promoting a charity initiative

Find out more about a charity initiative you're interested in supporting. Explain its purpose and why people should contribute money to it.

> I would like to raise money to give out water rollers in developing countries. In some countries, people—usually women—have to walk a long way to reach clean water. Often, they carry it home in containers on their heads. Giving the women water rollers would allow them to carry seven or eight times more water in a single trip. This would …

The Hippo Water Roller makes it easier for rural communities in Africa to transport water.

Presentation 2

MODEL PRESENTATION

A Complete the transcript of the presentation using the words in the box.

made up	fulfilling	had climbed	to climb
suffered	make it	draw on	might

"You'll die up there. You'll never ¹_____."

That's what everyone said when I told them I wanted ²_____ Mount Everest. I'm happy to say I proved them wrong.

My name is Richard, and I've always loved the outdoors. By the time I turned 30, I ³_____ over 100 mountains. Last year, I joined an expedition to climb Mount Everest. Many people doubted me and said that I wasn't ready for Everest yet. But I had ⁴_____ my mind, and nothing was going to change it.

I trained hard for the climb. But after the expedition began, I quickly realized that nothing can prepare you for the conditions on Everest. It's easy for accidents to happen when you're not getting enough oxygen to your muscles at high altitudes. At one point, I slipped and dropped my goggles, which are safety glasses that protect the eyes from harmful UV rays. I ⁵_____ from snow blindness for a few days. Imagine you have something in your eye and your vision is blurry. Your eyes ⁶_____ feel like they're burning. That's what it felt like for me.

I had to ⁷_____ all my mental strength to reach the summit of Mount Everest. It was the hardest thing I've ever done, but also the most ⁸_____. Thanks for listening.

B ▶ **P.2** Watch the presentation and check your answers.

C ▶ **P.2** Review the list of presentation skills from Units 1–6 below. Which does the speaker use? Check (✓) them as you watch again. Then compare with a partner.

The speaker …
- ☐ asks the audience questions
- ☐ asks the audience to imagine themselves in a particular situation
- ☐ uses examples the audience is familiar with
- ☐ uses props
- ☐ begins with a strong statement
- ☐ explains technical words that the audience may not understand

YOUR TURN

A You are going to plan and give a short presentation about your most significant achievement. It can be school-related, or something from your personal life. Make notes in the chart below.

> What achievement are you most proud of?
>
>
> Who or what helped you achieve this goal?
>
>
> Why does this achievement mean so much to you?

B Look at the useful phrases in the box below. Think about which ones you will need in your presentation.

> **Useful phrases**
>
> | | |
> |---|---|
> | **Using time expressions:** | *When I was … years old, …*
 Last year, … |
> | **Talking about past goals:** | *I wanted to …*
 My goal was to … |
> | **Describing an achievement:** | *I managed to …*
 … helped me achieve my goal of … |

C Work with a partner. Take turns giving your presentation using your notes. Use some of the presentation skills from Units 1–6 below. As you listen, check (✓) each skill your partner uses.

> The speaker …
> - ☐ asks the audience questions
> - ☐ asks the audience to imagine themselves in a particular situation
> - ☐ uses examples the audience is familiar with
> - ☐ uses props
> - ☐ begins with a strong statement
> - ☐ explains technical words that the audience may not understand

D Give your partner some feedback on their talk. Include at least two things you liked and one thing that could be improved.

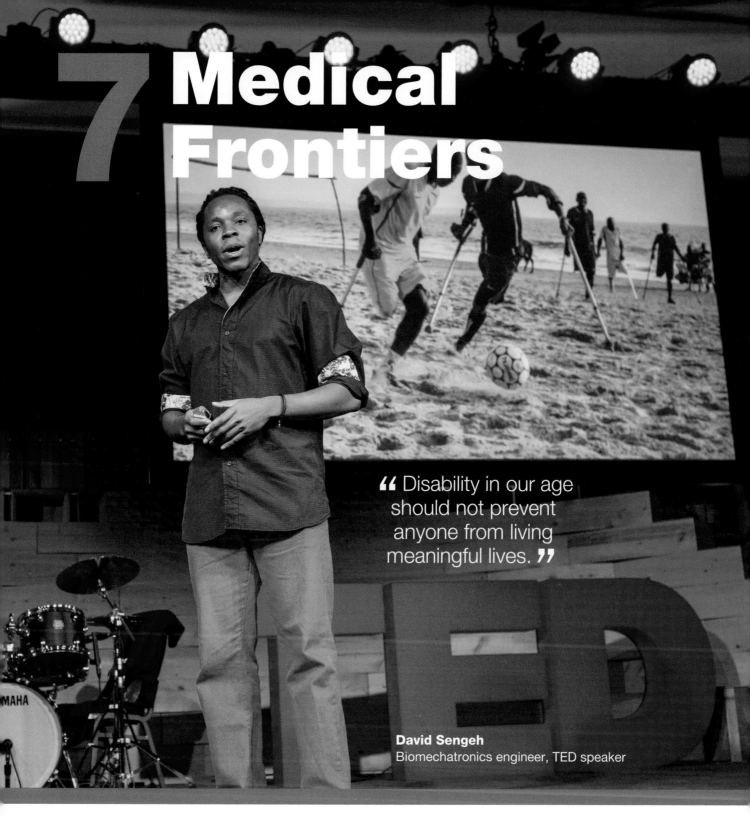

7 Medical Frontiers

" Disability in our age should not prevent anyone from living meaningful lives. "

David Sengeh
Biomechatronics engineer, TED speaker

UNIT GOALS

In this unit, you will ...

- talk about medical discoveries.
- read about the medical uses of 3-D printing.
- watch a TED Talk about a medical innovation.

WARM UP

▶ **7.1** Watch part of David Sengeh's TED Talk. Answer the questions with a partner.

1 What are some challenges that people with disabilities might face?

2 How do you think David Sengeh is addressing these challenges?

A prosthetic leg helps its wearer get around more easily.

7A Innovation

VOCABULARY The language of discovery

A Read the paragraph below. Then match the base form of each **bold** word to its definition.

Many medical discoveries have made our lives better. Some have been drugs; others have been technologies. For example, Dr. Alexander Fleming saved millions of lives when he **discovered** penicillin, a drug that kills bacteria. In 1976, Dean Kamen **invented** the insulin pump. This modern **innovation** is **designed** to make life easier for people with diabetes by removing the need for daily insulin injections. The work of these scientists and inventors have contributed greatly to the area of science and medicine.

1 discover ○   ○ to make changes or improvements to an existing product or idea

2 invent ○   ○ to form a plan, sketch, or model of something

3 innovate ○   ○ to create something that never existed before

4 design ○   ○ to find something that exists, but that no one knew about before

B Complete the sentences. Circle the correct words.

1 Al-Zahrawi, a doctor who lived in Spain during the 10th and 11th centuries, (**invented** / **discovered**) many surgical instruments and procedures.

2 Architects (**design** / **innovate**) all kinds of buildings, including hotels and hospitals.

3 One of Galileo Galilei's contributions to science was his (**innovation** / **discovery**) of four of Jupiter's moons.

C Work with a partner. Can you think of any other famous scientists and inventors?

90

LISTENING Drug discovery and development

> **Detecting signpost language**
>
> Signpost words and phrases tell the listener what has just happened and what is going to happen next.
>
> *I'm going to focus on …*   *Let's turn to …*   *We've looked at …*

A ▷ **7.2** Watch biotech executive Michael Hanley talk about his research in diabetes. What is a "first in class" drug?

   a a drug that uses a completely new approach to treat a condition

   b a drug that is superior to existing treatments

B ▷ **7.3** Watch and circle **T** for true or **F** for false.

   1 Symlin and Byetta treat different forms of diabetes.   **T**   **F**

   2 Both Symlin and Byetta are based on a human hormone.   **T**   **F**

   3 The FDA decides whether to approve or reject a new drug.   **T**   **F**

C CRITICAL THINKING

Analyzing **What are some commercial advantages of developing a "first in class" drug? Discuss with a partner.**

Dr. Michael Hanley has worked in the biotech sector for many years.

SPEAKING Improving lives

A ▷ **7.4** What is Speaker B's innovation for treating diabetes?

A: What made you decide to study medicine?

B: My sister, actually. She has diabetes, and I've seen how tough it is for her. I want to help people with diabetes live better lives.

A: I didn't know your sister has diabetes. Does she have to give herself insulin injections every day?

B: She used to. Now she uses an insulin pump. It's great because it's less painful and it delivers insulin more accurately than injections. Unfortunately, it's also pretty expensive.

A: Are there any other treatment options?

B: Yes, there are. In fact, my research focuses on designing insulin patches, which should make dealing with diabetes cheaper and safer.

A: Wow, that's great! I think that will be really useful for diabetics. I hope your research is successful.

B Practice the conversation with a partner.

C Work with a partner. Talk about the benefits of a drug or medical device. Use the expressions in blue above to help you.

> I think asthma inhalers are great because …

> I agree. They're small and easy to carry, so they make dealing with asthma …

LANGUAGE FOCUS Making predictions, expectations, and guesses

A ▶ **7.5** Study the timeline of future advances in medicine. Which technologies are you familiar with? Tell a partner.

FUTURE MEDICAL TECHNOLOGIES
Enormous technological changes in medicine and healthcare are heading our way.

2022
Nanoparticles might be able to deliver medication directly to cancer cells to make cancer treatments less painful.

2024
Wearable devices could communicate information such as your heart rate and blood pressure directly to your doctor.

2045
Robots could replace nurses in hospitals; they will lift patients and help in surgery.

2122
Thanks to advances in medicine, people could start living to **age 150**.

150

2062
Contact lenses that give people superhuman eyesight may allow users to zoom in on objects and see in the dark.

B ▶ **7.6** Listen to an explanation of nanotechnology. What are some medical uses of nanoparticles?

C ▶ **7.7** Watch and study the language in the chart.

Making predictions

People will communicate with their doctors without leaving home in the future.
Robots should be able to do nurses' jobs in the future.

People could live to age 150 by 2122, but I doubt it.
I doubt that people will live to age 150 by 2122.

Do you think robots will replace nurses in the future?
Yes, I think robots are likely to replace nurses in the future.

For more information on **modals of probability**, see Grammar Summary 7 on page 186.

D ▶ **7.6** Listen to the explanation in **B** again. Complete the sentences from the explanation.

1 "Researchers are also hopeful that nanoparticles _____ one day _____ to treat diabetes by delivering insulin to targeted cells."

2 "In addition, nanoparticles _____ to deliver vaccines in the future."

3 "It _____ therefore _____ a big difference to public health, particularly in the developing world."

E Complete the conversation. Circle the correct words.

A: Technology allows us to treat a greater number of illnesses these days.

B: Yeah. I think advances in technology ¹(**will** / **might**) definitely enable us to live longer in the future.

A: How can you be so sure?

B: Well, my dad's a doctor and he says nanoparticles ²(**could** / **should**) be able to cure serious diseases. Also, in the future, scientists ³(**doubt that they will** / **are likely to**) grow organs in labs. In fact, some doctors have already done this.

A: Do you think people ⁴(**will** / **should**) visit the doctor less often?

B: I'm not sure. It's possible. It's also possible that in a few years, nurses ⁵(**might** / **should**) be replaced by robots. But I doubt it. I think nurses ⁶(**may** / **will**) always be around.

F Answer the questions. Then share your answers with a partner and explain why you are certain/uncertain about them.

1 Do you think superhuman eyesight will be possible in the future?

_____

2 How likely do you think it is that people will live longer in the future?

_____

SPEAKING Talking about future technology

A Work in a small group. Look at the list of possible future technologies on the right. Brainstorm what problem each one might solve or what purpose it might have.

B Choose the innovation you think will be the most important. Explain the reasons for your choice to your group members.

> I think stem-cell technology is the most important because it could cure diseases like …

> I disagree. I think exoskeleton suits will be the most important innovation because they will …

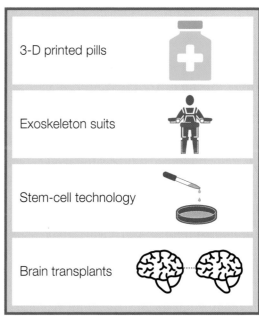

3-D printed pills

Exoskeleton suits

Stem-cell technology

Brain transplants

7C Just press "print"

PRE-READING Skimming

Skim the passage. The main purpose of the passage is to _____.

a explain the uses of a technology

b express an opinion about a technology

c describe the advantages and disadvantages of a technology

▶ 7.8

1   Imagine being able to print rocket engine parts,
chocolate figurines, designer sunglasses, or
even pizzas—just by pressing a single button. It
may sound like something out of science fiction, but
5   it's increasingly becoming a reality.

Thanks to 3-D printing, companies are
reimagining their long-term business plans. General
Electric, for example, is already using 3-D printers
to make some parts of jet engines. Airbus envisions
10 that by 2050, entire planes could be built out of
3-D printed parts. And this trend isn't just limited
to corporate giants. Dutch architectural firm DUS is
3-D printing a house on the banks of Amsterdam's
Buiksloter Canal.

15 **THE ADVANTAGES OF 3-D PRINTING**

Invented in the mid-1980s, 3-D printers create solid,
three-dimensional objects from various materials
such as plastic, wax, wood, gold, or titanium.[1] A
major advantage of 3-D printing is that designs for
20 objects can be easily **customized** or changed.
When designs change in **traditional** manufacturing,
the machinery that makes the objects needs to be
redesigned or upgraded, which can be very costly.
But in the case of 3-D printers, only the software
25 needs to be **modified**.

3-D printing is also better than traditional
manufacturing because there's no wasted material.
With traditional manufacturing, material is cut away
to create an object, but 3-D printing uses only what
30 is necessary. Guided by software, a 3-D printer
builds an object one layer at a time, placing material
only where it needs to be. As a result, it can make
complex objects less expensively.

MEDICAL USES OF 3-D PRINTING

35 This precision is making it possible to produce
things that have never been made before. A team
of Harvard University researchers recently printed
human tissue, complete with blood vessels—a
crucial step toward one day transplanting human
40 organs printed from a patient's own cells. "That's
the ultimate goal of 3-D bio-printing," says Jennifer
Lewis, who led the research. "We are many years
away from achieving this goal."

A young boy with a hand malformation tries on his new 3-D printed hand.

3-D printers can create bones, organs,
45 **synthetic** skin, and prosthetic[2] body parts—such
as hands and arms. In fact, 3-D printing saved a
dying baby named Kaiba Gionfriddo, who was born
with a condition that regularly caused the airways
near his lungs to collapse. Using a 3-D printer, a
50 team of researchers in the United States printed a
flexible tube, which they implanted[3] in Kaiba, and
which enabled him to breathe on his own.

3-D printing also provided a nose for an Irish
baby, Tessa Evans, who was born without one.
55 Over time, 3-D printed implants of increasing sizes
will be surgically placed under her skin where
her nose should be. The implants will gradually
create a "nose" from her own skin, allowing her
to look just like everyone else as she grows into
60 adulthood. If it weren't for 3-D printing, doctors
would have had an extremely difficult time

modeling the implant and customizing it to suit
Tessa's face.

THE FUTURE OF 3-D PRINTING

65 Clearly, 3-D printing has much potential for growth.
While there is no doubt that this medical technology
will continue to improve many people's lives, the
challenge lies in developing software that is advanced
or sophisticated enough to create the initial blueprints.
70 Designing the blueprint or a digital model for a vital
organ—with all its cell types and structures—is an
extremely complex process. Nevertheless, many are
hopeful that this obstacle will soon be overcome, and
that 3-D printing will change the face of medicine.

[1] **titanium:** *n.* a very hard metal
[2] **prosthetic:** *adj.* artificial
[3] **implanted:** *v.* inserted into the body

UNDERSTANDING MAIN IDEAS

Choose the sentence that best describes the author's attitude toward 3-D printing.

    a This technology will be of more benefit to corporate giants like General Electric than to smaller start-ups.

    b Medical uses of this technology will make life easier for many people.

    c Applications in engineering, such as manufacturing airplanes, are currently the most important use of this technology.

UNDERSTANDING DETAILS

Complete the Venn diagram using the information below.

    a cuts objects from material

    b runs on software

    c can be expensive to upgrade

    d is easy to customize

    e makes three-dimensional objects

    f tends to create waste

3-D printing   Traditional manufacturing

BUILDING VOCABULARY

A Complete the sentences. Circle the correct words from the passage.

    1 With 3-D printing technology, the process of making prosthetic devices is quicker and cheaper than with (**traditional** / **three-dimensional**) methods.

    2 The prosthetic arm was (**customized** / **synthetic**) to match the wearer's favorite color: purple.

    3 As more companies start to use 3-D printing, their business strategies will need to be (**customized** / **modified**).

    4 Playing (**synthetic** / **three-dimensional**) video games is fun because they are more realistic.

    5 Wigs made from human hair usually look more natural than wigs made from (**synthetic** / **customized**) hair.

B CRITICAL THINKING

Evaluating 3-D printing is making it possible to produce things that have never been made before, like replacement bones and organs. Do you think this could raise any ethical or moral issues? Discuss with a partner.

7D The sore problem of prosthetic limbs

TEDTALKS

DAVID SENGEH grew up in Sierra Leone, where many people underwent **amputation** of their **limbs** during the country's civil war. Sengeh noticed that a lot of these people weren't wearing their prostheses. When he found out why, Sengeh realized that the **conventional** way of making artificial body parts wasn't working, and he decided to do something about it.

David Sengeh's idea worth spreading is that those who have a **disability** should have the opportunity to live active, enjoyable lives—beginning with more comfortable prosthetics.

PREVIEWING

Read the paragraphs above. Circle the correct meaning of each **bold** word. You will hear these words in the TED Talk.

1 In an **amputation**, a part of the body is (**cut off** / **replaced**), either surgically or as the result of an accident or injury.

2 Your **limbs** are your (**fingers and toes** / **arms and legs**).

3 If something is **conventional**, it's based on an (**uncommon** / **accepted**) way of doing things.

4 **Disability** is a (**physical or mental condition** / **side effect**) that limits a person's movements, senses, or activities.

VIEWING

A ▶ 7.9 Watch Part 1 of the TED Talk. Circle **T** for true, **F** for false, or **NG** for not given.

1 David Sengeh had to flee with his family during the war in Sierra Leone.　　　　T　　F　　NG

2 One of Sengeh's family members is an amputee.　　　　T　　F　　NG

3 After the war, David Sengeh was troubled when he saw how some amputees were using their prostheses incorrectly.　　　　T　　F　　NG

4 Many amputees found their prosthetic limbs painful to wear because they didn't fit well.　　　　T　　F　　NG

B ▶ **7.10** Watch Part 2 of the TED Talk. Match the labels to the images that show how David Sengeh creates custom prosthetic sockets.

Finite Element Modeling	Prosthetic Socket	Magnetic Resonance Imaging
○	○	○
○	○	○

C Match the descriptions (**a–c**) to the images in **B**.

a Sengeh creates a customized, multi-material prosthesis using a 3-D printer.

b Sengeh captures the actual shape of the patient's anatomy.

c Sengeh predicts where pressure points on the socket will be.

D ▶ **7.11** Watch Part 3 of the TED Talk. Choose the correct options.

1 Which of the following is NOT mentioned by Sengeh?

a We need to remove the negative stereotype associated with wearing prostheses.

b We need to create comfortable and affordable prostheses.

c We need to make functional prostheses more readily available around the world.

2 Which sentence best paraphrases the following quote from the talk?

"Whether it's in Sierra Leone or in Boston, I hope this not only restores but indeed transforms their sense of human potential."

a Sengeh hopes that the work he's doing will make people more interested in helping others.

b Sengeh hopes his work will help people become the best versions of themselves.

c Sengeh feels that people in poor countries need his work more than people in wealthy countries.

E **CRITICAL THINKING**

Evaluating How do you think Sengeh's prostheses can help amputees heal psychologically? Discuss with a partner.

VOCABULARY IN CONTEXT

A ▶ **7.12** Watch the excerpts from the TED Talk. Choose the correct meaning of the words.

B Complete the sentences with the words from the box.

infamous	go through	intolerable	interface

1 That restaurant is _____ for its poor service.

2 The heat and humidity in the summer can be _____ .

3 In order to get a job, you have to _____ an interview selection process.

4 The well-designed _____ of this app makes searching for information easy.

PRESENTATION SKILLS Body movement and gestures

Your body language and gestures can reinforce your listeners' understanding of your message, or they can distract.

• Try to keep calm. Avoid nervous body language like swaying.

• Gesture with your palms out and open.

• Use arm and hand movements that help to illustrate your message.

A ▶ **7.13** Watch part of David Sengeh's TED Talk. Check (✓) the gestures he makes with his hands.

☐ He claps his hands.   ☐ He gestures with his palms open.

☐ He puts his hands in his pockets.   ☐ He points to a slide in his presentation.

B Work with a partner. Brainstorm other positive body movements and gestures.

7E Inventing solutions

COMMUNICATE Pitching an invention

A Work with a partner. "Invent" a technology that would make life easier, more enjoyable, or more comfortable for a disabled person or a person with a particular illness. Consider the following questions.

What is your invention?	What problem does it solve?	How does it work?
Who is it designed for?	What does it look like?	How much does it cost?

B With your partner, pitch your invention to the class. You may want to use visuals like posters.

> **Using persuasive language**
> *Without a doubt, …*   *It's certain that …*
> *For these reasons, …*   *Not only is it able to … , it also …*

C As a class, vote on the best pitch.

WRITING A persuasive letter

Choose either your own invention or one of the inventions that the other pairs in your class presented. Write a letter to a potential investor describing what it does and why it is worth investing in.

> Dear Mr. Smith,
> My name is _____ . I am writing to inform you
> of my latest invention. I have invented a new kind of wheelchair
> that can climb stairs. When the user pushes a button, …

The iBot, a special wheelchair created by Dean Kamen

8 Life Decisions

" ... claiming your 20s is one of the simplest, yet most transformative, things you can do for work, for love, for your happiness. "

Meg Jay
Clinical psychologist, TED speaker

UNIT GOALS

In this unit, you will ...

- talk about important life events.
- read about decisions that define your life.
- watch a TED Talk about the importance of your 20s.

WARM UP

▶ 8.1 Watch part of Meg Jay's TED Talk. Answer the questions with a partner.

1 What do you think Meg Jay means by "claiming your 20s"?

2 When do you think is the best time in life to get married or have children?

High school students
from Connecticut, U.S., at
their graduation ceremony

8A Entering adulthood

VOCABULARY Describing milestones in life

A Read the paragraph below. Then match each **bold** phrase to its definition.

A Pew Research Center study in the United States compared Millennials (people born between 1981–1996)
with the Silent Generation (people born between 1928–1945). The study showed that many more Millennial
women are **getting degrees** and **pursuing careers** than Silent Generation women did in their young
adult years. In 1963—when they were aged 18 to 33—only 38 percent of Silent Generation women were
employed; today, 63 percent of Millennial women are employed. Furthermore, fewer young adults today are
settling down compared to their Silent Generation counterparts. According to the study, financial concerns
are causing many young people to **put off** owning a home and **raising a family**.

1 getting a degree ○	○	working hard in a profession
2 pursuing a career ○	○	getting married or finding a permanent place to live
3 settling down ○	○	taking care of children while they are growing up
4 put off ○	○	completing a college or university course
5 raising a family ○	○	delay

B Which of the following would you like to do in the future? Check (✓) your answers.

☐ get married   ☐ get a job   ☐ live overseas

☐ buy a house   ☐ have children   ☐ get a degree

C Compare your answers in **B** with a partner. Give reasons for your choices.

LISTENING Comparing generations

> **Listening for opinions**
> Words like *think*, *believe*, *feel*, and *in my opinion* are used to express beliefs and opinions. They can help you decide if you agree or disagree with the speaker.

A ▶ **8.2** Watch Professor Laurence Steinberg talk about adolescence. Check (✓) the milestones he reached by the time he turned 25.

- ☐ finished his formal education
- ☐ got a job
- ☐ started his own business
- ☐ was financially independent
- ☐ got engaged
- ☐ became a parent

Dr. Laurence Steinberg, author of the best-selling book *Age of Opportunity*

B ▶ **8.3** Watch the rest of the interview. Is Dr. Steinberg worried about today's young people? Why or why not?

C CRITICAL THINKING

Reflecting Look at your answers in **A**. Do you think 25 is an appropriate age to reach these milestones? Discuss with a partner.

SPEAKING Talking about adult responsibilities

A ▶ **8.4** Do you agree with Speaker A or Speaker B? Why?

A: Did you hear Anne's brother is about to become a father?

B: Yeah, I heard. Exciting, right?

A: Don't you think he's kind of young to be a parent?

B: Well, he's 27 already. I think that's a good age to start raising a family.

A: Really? Do you think you'll be ready to be a parent at 27?

B: I think so. I love children, and I can't wait to have one of my own. What about you?

A: For me, 27 is way too young.

B: Why?

A: Because I'll have just started my career at that age, and I'll still be paying off my school loans, too. I want to be more financially secure before I have any kids.

B Practice the conversation with a partner.

C Work with a partner. What do you think is a good age to start living on your own? Use the expressions in blue above to help you.

> I think 20 is a good age to start living on your own.

> I disagree. I think you should … before you start living on your own.

8B Plans and aspirations

LANGUAGE FOCUS Making plans for the future

A ▶ **8.5** Read about aspirations of young adults after they finish college. Do any of the aspirations below match your own? Tell a partner.

ASPIRATIONS OF COLLEGE STUDENTS

Here's what most young adults would like to do after they finish college.

31% Become financially stable

28% Secure a dream job

10% Get married

10% Go to graduate school

2% Become a business owner

2% Buy a house

4% Start a family

6% Travel

8% Pay off student loans

B ▶ **8.6** Listen to the conversation. What aspirations does Ian have?

C ▶ **8.7** Watch and study the language in the chart.

Talking about milestones
By this time next year, Ian will have paid off his loan. I'll have gone to graduate school by then. By the time they turn 20, the twins will have moved out of their parents' house.
Next year, I'll have been working here for five years. When Dave turns 30, he'll have been living on his own for ten years. When Jack and Kate get married, they will have been dating for four years.
Won't Emma have graduated from college by then? How long will you have been studying when you graduate?

For more information on the **future perfect** and **future perfect progressive**, see Grammar Summary 8 on page 186.

D ▶ **8.6** Listen to the conversation in **B** again. Complete the sentences from the conversation.

1 "When do you think _____ your loans?"

2 "Hopefully, _____ enough money by the time I start my trip."

3 "By the time I graduate, _____ Mandarin for six years."

E ▶ **8.8** Complete the information using the correct form of the words in parentheses. Then listen and check your answers.

By the time they reach retirement age, most of today's American Millennials ^1_____ (**work**) for over 40 years. But ^2_____ they _____ (**save**) enough money by then? According to Alexandra Mondalek, writing in *Time* magazine, Millennials are saving more money than any other generation. Even so, the majority of Americans still ^3_____ (**will not save**) enough to retire comfortably. This explains why more and more Millennials think they will be forced to put off retirement. Many young homeowners are planning to work well into their 70s, as they expect that they ^4_____ (**will not pay off**) their mortgages before then.

The office of the Society of Grownups, a company that provides financial advice to Millennials

SPEAKING When will you ...?

A Complete your plans and aspirations in the timeline below.

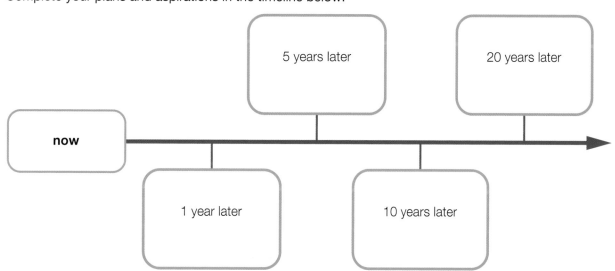

- now
- 1 year later
- 5 years later
- 10 years later
- 20 years later

B Share your timeline with a partner. Compare your partner's plans and aspirations with your own. Discuss any similarities or differences that you notice.

By this time next year, I'll have ...

Really? That's too soon for me. I don't plan to ... for another five years or so.

8C The defining decade

Look at the photo. What decade of your life do you think is the most important?

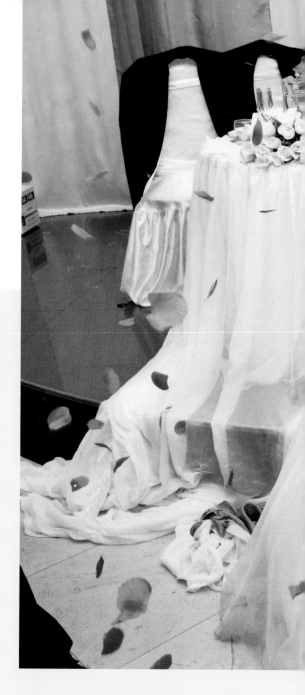

▶ 8.9

1   For the longest time, adulthood—and the responsibilities that come with it—was thought to begin in your 20s. After finishing school, 20-something-year-olds were expected to
5 be independent, start careers, and raise families. Many of today's youth, however, are now delaying marriage, careers, children, and other milestones of adulthood. In the last few years, the media has romanticized this phenomena, coining phrases like
10 "30 is the new 20" and "kidulthood." As society has begun to believe that it's OK for young adults to put off commitments, it's now increasingly acceptable for today's 20-somethings to work at low-level jobs and to live with their parents. Many "kidults" are leaving
15 serious decisions about work, marriage, and family until later, when they're in their 30s.

    Psychologist and TED speaker Meg Jay felt this way about her 20s, too, until she had what she calls an "aha" moment.[1] What changed her mind?
20 A 26-year-old woman named Alex. A 20-something herself, Jay was just starting her career as a counselor when Alex came to see her. Alex wanted advice on how to deal with her "knucklehead" boyfriend. Jay didn't consider Alex's problem to be
25 serious; however, her supervisor pointed out that maybe Alex had a more complex problem. Perhaps Alex wasn't taking her relationships seriously enough. In other words, even though Alex knew she was with a person who wasn't good enough for
30 her, she might still end up marrying him or someone similar. "The best time to work on Alex's marriage," the supervisor said, "is before she has one."

Jay realized at that moment that the 20s aren't a time for **coasting**, but rather, the best
35 time to be making serious choices about the future and preparing for adulthood. She points out that 80 percent of life's most **defining moments** take place by age 35. This means that eight out of ten of life's important decisions and experiences
40 will have happened by your mid-30s. Jay refers to research that backs this up:[2]
- Female fertility **peaks** at age 28.
- More than half of Americans are married to or dating their future partners by the age of 30.
45 - Approximately 70 percent of lifetime wage growth happens in the first ten years of a career.

A couple in Pankisi Gorge, Georgia, cuts their wedding cake.

- The brain ends its final growth spurt[3] in the 20s, as it begins to rewire[4] itself for adulthood. This means that if you want to change something
50 about yourself, your 20s is a good time to do it.

According to Jay, "[American] culture has 'trivialized' young adulthood," reinforcing the message that it's OK to extend adolescence. In an interview with National Public Radio, Jay said
55 that more and more people these days suffer from "present bias." In other words, they place more value on immediate rewards than on achieving long-term goals. But Jay is hopeful that more 20-somethings will start thinking ahead. A lot of what she does with
60 her 20-something clients is to ask them specific questions about the future, such as where they hope they will be in five or ten years, if they want children, or what type of job they hope to get. She believes that in order to pursue a happier, more fulfilling future,
65 what's important is not only thinking about these things, but thinking about them at the right stage of your life. And in Jay's opinion, the critical period for adult development is actually in your 20s.

[1] an "aha" moment: n. a situation in which a person has an important realization
[2] back something up: v. to support it
[3] growth spurt: n. a period when a thing or a person grows a lot in a short period of time
[4] rewire: v. to change the connections between neurons in the brain

UNDERSTANDING MAIN IDEAS

Which sentence best summarizes the main idea of the passage?

a Many people in their 20s are unable to handle the responsibilities that come with adulthood.

b The 20s are an important time to make decisions about the future because many important social and biological milestones occur during that period.

c We are currently experiencing serious social problems because the media has convinced young people that their 20s aren't important.

UNDERSTANDING DETAILS

Match each expression to the point it is used to describe.

1 "Thirty is the new 20."　　　○　　　○ People in their 20s should take their current relationships more seriously.

2 "The best time to work on Alex's ○　　　○ It's OK for people in their 20s to put off serious marriage is before she has one." commitments until later in life.

3 "Present bias"　　　　　　　○　　　○ Most people in their 20s don't have enough discipline or patience to plan ahead and wait for future rewards.

SCANNING FOR FACTS

Scan the passage to complete the facts below.

1 About 80 percent of major life decisions are made by age _____ .

2 Over _____ percent of Americans will have met their future partners by the time they turn 30.

3 In your _____ , your brain starts preparing you for adulthood.

BUILDING VOCABULARY

A Complete the sentences using the correct form of the words in blue from the passage.

1 Graduating from college is a(n) _____ for many people.

2 Neuroscientists now believe that intelligence can _____ at any time up to age 40.

3 Experts say that if you're just _____ at work, it's probably time to get a new job.

4 Some sociologists worry that reality TV shows such as *The Bachelor* _____ important life milestones, such as marriage.

5 I had to _____ my medical leave because I still wasn't feeling well enough for work.

B CRITICAL THINKING

Reflecting Jay asks her 20-something clients the following questions to help them think about the future. How would you answer these questions? Discuss with a partner.

1 Do you want children? If so, what do you hope to accomplish before you have children?

2 What type of job do you hope to get?

8D Why 30 is not the new 20

TEDTALKS

MEG JAY believes that young adults should be planning their lives more **consciously** than many of them are doing today. Exploration is OK in the 20s, she says, but unless it has a real focus, Jay considers it **procrastination**. To avoid having an **identity crisis** in your 20s, Jay recommends using the time to make an **investment** in yourself instead. She believes that new opportunities are more likely to come from people we don't know, rather than our **peers**.

Meg Jay's idea worth spreading is that the 20s are the defining decade of adulthood.

PREVIEWING

Read the paragraphs above. Circle the correct meaning of each **bold** word. You will hear these words in the TED Talk.

1 If you do something **consciously**, you do it (**with intention** / **carelessly**).

2 **Procrastination** is the act of (**forgetting** / **delaying**) something.

3 If you are having an **identity crisis**, you are unsure of (**your purpose in life** / **what to call someone**).

4 An **investment** refers to the (**time or effort** / **thought**) that you put into something.

5 Your **peers** are people who are (**similar to** / **different from**) you in age, rank, or ability.

VIEWING

A ▶ **8.10** Watch Part 1 of the TED Talk. Check (✓) the statements that are true about Emma.

- ☑ She was underemployed.
- ☐ She had a well-paying job.
- ☐ Her boyfriend didn't always treat her well.
- ☐ Her boyfriend was very ambitious.
- ☐ She had an unhappy childhood.
- ☐ She had negative feelings about her family.
- ☐ She had a serious health problem.
- ☐ She had nobody to rely on in a crisis.

B ▶ **8.11** Watch Part 2 of the TED Talk. Choose the correct paraphrase for each piece of advice Meg Jay gave to Emma.

1 "Get identity capital."

 a Develop your qualities and skills by getting some experience.

 b Become wealthier by putting your money into reliable investments.

2 "Explore work and make it count."

 a Try new things, but get a job that you're genuinely interested in.

 b Try new things, but only take jobs that pay well.

3 Connect with "weak ties."

 a Build close relationships with everyone you know.

 b Get in touch with people who aren't close to you, such as friends of friends.

4 "Pick your family."

 a Change your attitude toward the family you were born into.

 b Create your own family by choosing a partner and having children.

C Which of these pieces of advice is Meg Jay most likely to agree with?

 a Try your best to stay positive and be happy with your current situation.

 b Be honest with yourself and use all the information available to you to make decisions.

 c Don't take love and work too seriously—it will all work out in the end.

D ▶ **8.12** Watch Part 3 of the TED Talk. How did Emma follow Meg Jay's advice and turn her life around? Order the events from 1 to 4.

_____ She left her live-in boyfriend.

_____ She found a job at an art museum in another state.

_____ She found a suitable partner and got married.

_____ She found a distant contact in her address book.

E Meg Jay compares 20-somethings to airplanes taking off. What does she mean by this analogy?

 a Small actions and events can help transform and shape the lives of 20-somethings.

 b 20-somethings must be clear where they want to go in life and learn how to stay the course.

F **CRITICAL THINKING**

Evaluating/Reflecting **Discuss these questions with a partner.**

1 Who is Meg Jay's intended audience? Who does she want to convince that "30 is not the new 20"?

2 After watching Meg Jay's TED Talk, do you feel differently about your 20s or 30s? Which pieces of Jay's advice might apply to you or someone you know?

 I think my cousin would really benefit from watching Meg Jay's TED Talk.

 How so?

VOCABULARY IN CONTEXT

A ▶ **8.13** Watch the excerpts from the TED Talk. Choose the correct meaning of the words.

B Complete the sentences with the words from the box.

| collect | like-minded | inner circles | kill time |

1 I often _____ by reading magazines and listening to music.

2 After hearing the bad news, she paused for a moment to _____ herself.

3 Meg Jay encourages 20-somethings to form relationships beyond their _____ and broaden their life experiences.

4 A study by two colleges found that we are often more attracted to _____ people.

PRESENTATION SKILLS Using a case study

Using a case study—describing a particular person or situation—is a memorable way to support your ideas. Here are some ways to do this.

- Present the case study like a story, with a beginning, a middle, and an end.
- Give specific details. For example, give a clear picture of the people involved. Describe when and where the situation took place.
- Ask the audience questions.
- Include a quote.

A ▶ **8.14** Watch part of Meg Jay's TED Talk. Which of the techniques above does she use?

B Work with a partner. Why might giving a case study be better than presenting facts to support an argument? To help your discussion, think about the following questions.

1 What would Meg Jay's TED Talk be like if she only used study results or statistics instead of a case history?

2 What topics or arguments might be better supported by case studies than by facts, and vice versa?

8E Hard choices

COMMUNICATE Giving advice

A Work in a group. Discuss what advice you think Meg Jay would give to the following people.

Matt, 23: Matt works at entry level in a good company, but he doesn't love his job. He doesn't know whether he'll grow in this career. Matt lives with a group of friends who are unemployed. They spend most of their time playing video games, so they can't give good career advice. They often tease Matt for worrying about his job.

Rachel, 25: Rachel has been going out with Aaron, a boy she met in high school, for ten years. Neither Rachel nor Aaron has dated anyone else. They don't have much in common anymore, but Rachel doesn't have any reason to dislike Aaron. Aaron recently proposed to her, but she thinks she's too young to get married. She's not sure what to do.

Elena, 28: Elena works over 60 hours a week at a high-paying, high-pressure job. She loves her job, and the company loves her. She's pretty certain she'll get a promotion soon. Elena doesn't have time for dating. She's OK with the idea of getting married, but she's not sure if marriage is really for her. All her friends are getting married, and she's starting to feel the pressure.

> **Expressing opinions**
>
> *I think she'd suggest ...*   *She might say it's better to ...*
>
> *She'd probably recommend ...*   *I guess she'd advise him/her to ...*

B Compare your ideas with another group's.

WRITING An advice column

Imagine you write an advice column for a newspaper. Choose one of the three people above, and write a piece for your column giving your advice.

Dear Matt,

I'm sorry to hear that your friends aren't very supportive of your goals and ambitions.

I think you should find a new place to live and try to look elsewhere for new job

opportunities. Moving out would help you because ...

9 Technology and Innovation

" I'd like to tell you a little bit about the challenges in building these, and some of the terrific opportunities for applying this technology. **"**

Vijay Kumar
Roboticist, TED speaker

UNIT GOALS

In this unit, you will ...

- talk about robots and other innovative technologies.
- read about the advantages and disadvantages of drones.
- watch a TED Talk about the applications of tiny flying robots.

WARM UP

▶ **9.1** Watch part of Vijay Kumar's TED Talk. Answer the questions with a partner.

1 What do robots help us with today? Have you ever seen a robot at work?

2 What advantages do you think small robots have over large robots?

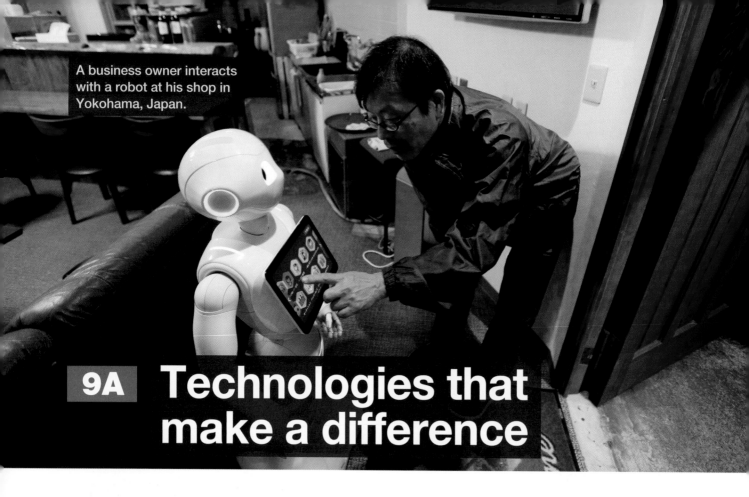

A business owner interacts with a robot at his shop in Yokohama, Japan.

9A Technologies that make a difference

VOCABULARY What can robots do?

A Read the paragraph below. Then match each **bold** word to its definition.

Robots are machines that we can **program** to handle repetitive or dangerous **functions**. For example, we use robots to **assemble** cars because they can do it more quickly and less expensively than humans. Also, because we can control them from a distance, **remote-controlled** robots can gather data and images from inaccessible places. For example, scientists can **operate** robots safely from dry land while they explore the ocean floor. Robots can also perform delicate tasks such as surgery. Using robots for surgery can sometimes be better than using human hands because robots can make tinier, more precise movements.

1 program ○ ○ uses

2 functions ○ ○ to make something work

3 assemble ○ ○ managed from far away

4 remote-controlled ○ ○ to put together

5 operate ○ ○ to write a set of instructions for a computer

B Complete the sentences using the words in **A**. One word is extra.

1 Robots often work in factories, where they _____ objects like cell phones.

2 Because a robot is a machine, it only does what we _____ it to do.

3 Robots can have many _____ , such as cleaning and doing industrial tasks.

4 _____ robots can go into areas that are dangerous for humans.

C Work with a partner. Would you trust a robot to perform surgery on you? Why or why not?

LISTENING Robobees

> **Drawing clues from context**
> Scientists often use jargon—technical terms used in specific areas of work or study—in presentations. When you hear scientific or technical jargon that you don't understand, try to work out the meaning from the context.

A ▶ **9.2** Watch roboticist Robert Wood talk about the types of robots he builds. Check (✓) the ways his robots are different from traditional robots.

- ☐ His robots are smaller.

- ☐ His robots are heavier.

- ☐ His robots move faster.

- ☐ His robots are easier to build and design.

B ▶ **9.2** Watch again. Discuss these questions.

1 Where does Wood get his ideas for his robots?

2 What kinds of applications might Wood's robots have in 20 years?

C CRITICAL THINKING

Reflecting If you could build a robot, what kind of robot would you want to build? Discuss with a partner.

Robert Wood builds robots that can work together.

SPEAKING Talking about technological devices

A ▶ **9.3** In what ways is Speaker B's device useful?

A: It's so hot today. I can't wait to go home and turn on the air conditioning.

B: Why don't you get a smart air conditioner? I got mine installed a few months ago.

A: A smart air conditioner? What's that?

B: It's an air conditioner that's connected to the Internet, so it can be controlled remotely. I usually turn it on using my smartphone while I'm out, so my house will be cool when I get home. It's great for hot days like today.

A: Sounds perfect! Is it easy to operate?

B: Yeah, it's really simple. It automatically turns off when I'm out. What I like most about it is that it can track usage over time and adjust its behavior. It's helped me reduce my electricity bill!

A: That sounds pretty cool. Can we go to your house now? I want to check it out!

B Practice the conversation with a partner.

C Work with a partner. Talk about your favorite device or technology and why it's useful. Use the expressions in blue above to help you.

My favorite tech device is my smart TV.

What does it do?

9B Driverless cars

LANGUAGE FOCUS Talking about advantages and disadvantages

A ▶ **9.4** Read about how driverless cars work. Would you like a driverless car? Why or why not?

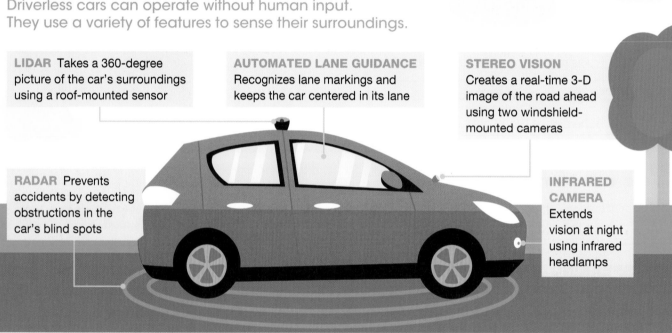

DRIVERLESS CARS

Driverless cars can operate without human input.
They use a variety of features to sense their surroundings.

LIDAR Takes a 360-degree picture of the car's surroundings using a roof-mounted sensor

AUTOMATED LANE GUIDANCE Recognizes lane markings and keeps the car centered in its lane

STEREO VISION Creates a real-time 3-D image of the road ahead using two windshield-mounted cameras

RADAR Prevents accidents by detecting obstructions in the car's blind spots

INFRARED CAMERA Extends vision at night using infrared headlamps

B ▶ **9.5** Listen to the conversation. Complete the sentences. Circle the correct words.

1 According to Jason, driverless cars will (**increase** / **reduce**) the likelihood of traffic jams.

2 Elizabeth is worried that the software in driverless cars might (**fail** / **collect personal information**).

C ▶ **9.6** Watch and study the language in the chart.

Talking about conditions
If you keep your eyes on the road, you'll be less likely to have an accident.
If you like to be in control, you won't like driverless cars.
Do you think more people will buy driverless cars if they become more affordable?
If I had a driverless car, I'd save money on insurance.
I'd buy a driverless car if there was no risk of malfunction.
If you had a driverless car, would you feel safe?

For more information on **first conditional** and **second conditional**, see Grammar Summary 9 on page 187.

D ▶ **9.5** Listen to the conversation in **B** again. Complete the sentences from the conversation.

1 "If I _____ a driverless car, _____ a lot more relaxed because I _____ to worry about parking."

2 "Also, if everyone _____ a driverless car, _____ less traffic."

3 "If the software _____, _____ probably _____ a car crash."

E Match the two parts of the sentences.

1 If more people had driverless cars, ○   ○ if they were equipped with better sensors.

2 If driverless cars become more popular, ○   ○ cities will need to be redesigned.

3 People will be more likely to buy driverless cars ○   ○ there would be fewer traffic accidents.

4 Driverless cars would be safer ○   ○ if costs come down.

F ▶ **9.7** Complete the information using the correct form of the words in parentheses. Then listen and check your answers.

Lyft—a private driving service—is planning to have an all-driverless car fleet by 2020. If it ¹_____ (**achieve**) this goal, it may be one of the first companies to have driverless taxis. Lyft is working with General Motors, which is currently developing driverless cars. If driverless car technology ²_____ (**be**) successful, taxi companies like Lyft ³_____ (**be**) able to reduce their operating costs significantly. Lyft will first test its vehicles in the United States. If customers use the service during the test period, they ⁴_____ (**be**) offered a choice of either a driverless car or a car with a human driver. However, for safety reasons, Lyft ⁵_____ (**have**) human drivers on board to take over if something goes wrong with the driverless vehicle.

A driverless pod from a transportation company in the U.K.

SPEAKING Discussing the impact of driverless cars

Work with a partner. How would cities be redesigned if everyone drove driverless cars? To help your discussion, consider the impact of driverless cars on the following.

traffic lights	road signs	parking lots

If everyone drove driverless cars, there would probably be ... because ...

9C Drones are here to stay

PRE-READING Skimming

Skim the passage. What are some benefits of drones? Check your answers with a partner.

▶ 9.8

1 Until recently, drones have generally been associated with military **surveillance**. Now, however, they are becoming easier for the average person to obtain; we may soon see them
5 replacing human labor in a variety of tasks. But are drones an important tool, or a danger to private citizens?

DRONES IN THE MILITARY

Drones, also known as unmanned aerial vehicles
10 (UAVs), are remotely controlled flying robots. Some drones are as small as birds, while others are the size of airplanes. Drones can carry instruments such as cameras and global positioning systems (GPS), and are used in situations where manned
15 flight is considered too risky or difficult. For example, they are commonly used by the military for intelligence-gathering, surveillance, and identifying targets.

OTHER DRONE USES

20 Apart from benefiting the military and law enforcement agencies, drones can help people perform **humanitarian** tasks. For instance, they can be used in disaster relief efforts to deliver blankets, clothing, and medical supplies to hard-to-reach
25 places. Furthermore, drones can be programmed to fly into the heart of storms—without any risk to human life—and gather important weather data. This information can help scientists predict natural disasters like hurricanes or tornadoes, and hopefully
30 save many lives in the process.

Camera-equipped drones can also produce maps that are much more detailed and accurate than those produced from satellite imagery. This will be a big help to conservation experts in mapping land use
35 changes such as deforestation, which is threatening an untold number of species. The U.S. government already uses drones to protect its lands and the species that inhabit them.

In addition, farmers can use drones to drop
40 fertilizers and pesticides[1] on crops. This not only saves money, but keeps farm workers safer by limiting their exposure to dangerous chemicals. Drone technology can also be used by farmers to monitor fields and find lost cattle. According to the Association
45 for Unmanned Vehicle Systems International (AUVSI), "Agriculture, far and away, is going to be the dominant market for UAV operations."

PRIVACY AND SAFETY ISSUES

Drones can be equipped with infrared sensors
50 which use temperature variations to "see" things

A drone flying over Dallas, Texas

the naked eye cannot detect. While this is helpful for getting a bird's eye view of a disaster or conflict zone, it could also be used by law enforcement agencies to spy on **civilians**. With thousands of
55 remote-controlled drones set to take to the skies over the United States, many people are concerned about privacy. The American Civil Liberties Union (ACLU) is worried that drones may be linked with cell phone tracking software[2] in the future, which
60 would enable law enforcement agencies to **carry out** surveillance on U.S. citizens and monitor people's movements.

Safety is another major concern. Anyone—from terrorists to criminals—can get their hands
65 on a drone. And even when controlled by skilled operators with good intentions, drones **pose a hazard**. Since 2001, there have been hundreds of military drone accidents worldwide. Even people in favor of drones feel that lack of safety is one of their
70 biggest **drawbacks**. Think of drones accidentally landing in backyards or, worse, crashing into

commercial planes. In April 2016, a British Airways aircraft was just about to land at Heathrow Airport when it collided with a drone. There have been
75 several similar instances already.

DRONES AND REGULATION

The ongoing debate over drones suggests that we are in the midst of a "drone fever." The most important question going forward is how
80 governments and agencies will regulate this technology to make sure it benefits, rather than harms, individuals and societies. As drones become more common, the importance of ensuring safe and responsible use will no doubt
85 become greater.

---

[1] **fertilizers and pesticides:** *n.* chemicals used in farming; fertilizers help plants grow, and pesticides kill insects
[2] **cell phone tracking software:** *n.* software installed on a cell phone that indicates the phone's location

UNDERSTANDING MAIN IDEAS

Which of the following sentences would the author agree with?

   a Although drones can be useful, the disadvantages far outweigh the advantages.

   b Drones may be able to improve our lives, but there are issues that need to be addressed first.

   c Due to safety reasons, only governments and agencies should be allowed to operate drones.

UNDERSTANDING DETAILS

Complete the chart showing the pros and cons of drones.

Pros	Cons
1 Can help the _____ gather intelligence and identify targets	**1** Could be used to spy on civilians by connecting with _____
2 Can be used to _____ disaster relief items to victims of natural disasters	**2** Easy access to drones means that dangerous people like _____ or _____ can get one
3 Able to use weather data to _____ natural disasters	**3** Drones have caused many _____
4 Can track wildlife and map changes in _____	
5 Can make farm jobs _____ by reducing workers' contact with harmful chemicals	

BUILDING VOCABULARY

A Match the words in blue from the passage to their definitions.

   1 surveillance ○   ○ disadvantages

   2 humanitarian ○   ○ to do; to conduct

   3 civilians ○   ○ to be dangerous

   4 carry out ○   ○ monitoring someone closely

   5 pose a hazard ○   ○ ordinary citizens

   6 drawbacks ○   ○ devoted to the improvement of people's welfare

B CRITICAL THINKING

Evaluating In your opinion, is widespread civilian use of drones unavoidable? Discuss with a partner.

In my opinion, it'll be difficult to stop people from using drones. They're already quite common.

Yeah, but I think there needs to be stricter rules on ...

9D Robots that fly ... and cooperate

TEDTALKS

VIJAY KUMAR's robots can do jobs that are too difficult or dangerous for humans. For example, they can act as **first responders** in disaster situations; they can **assess** dangerous situations before humans get involved. Several of Kumar's robots can work **cooperatively**, allowing them to increase their strength and abilities. They can also be fitted with cameras that show them where **obstacles** are.

Vijay Kumar's idea worth spreading is that agile, **autonomous** robots can help humans respond to disasters, perform difficult physical tasks, and much more.

PREVIEWING

Read the paragraphs above. Match each **bold** word to its meaning. You will hear these words in the TED Talk.

1 evaluate _____

2 done in a manner that involves working together _____

3 independent; self-controlling _____

4 things that get in the way _____

5 people trained to provide immediate assistance in an emergency _____

VIEWING

A ▶ **9.9** Watch Part 1 of the TED Talk. Check (✓) the ways Kumar's robots can be used.

☐ They can design buildings.

☐ They can look for dangerous leaks.

☐ They can be used to transport goods.

☐ They can work together to carry heavy objects.

☐ They can be used to prevent natural disasters.

☐ They can assess the damage after natural disasters.

B The diagram below illustrates the robots' motions—how they move. Match each description to the correct stage in the diagram. Write **a**, **b**, or **c**.

    a The robot changes its orientation.

    b The robot builds up momentum to start moving.

    c The robot recovers and hovers in the air.

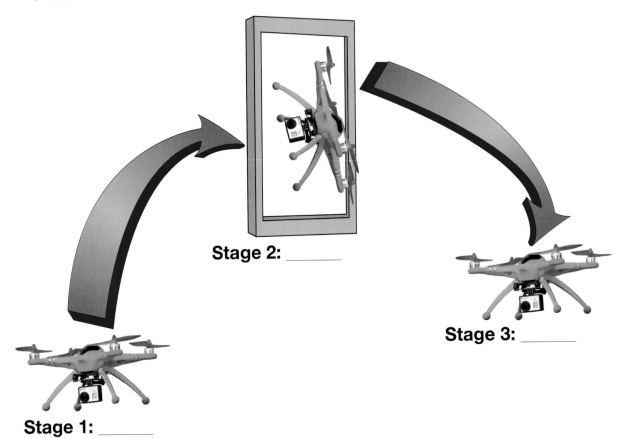

Stage 2: _____

Stage 3: _____

Stage 1: _____

C ▶ **9.10** Watch Part 2 of the TED Talk. Then look at the picture on page 123. Discuss the questions below with a partner.

    1 What are the ants in the picture doing?

    2 What aspect of ant behavior does Kumar want his robots to have?

D ▶ **9.11** Watch Part 3 of the TED Talk. If a drone is entering a building for the first time, can it complete its mission under the following conditions? Circle **Y** for yes or **N** for no.

    1 The drone is not connected to GPS but has a map of the building.   **Y**   **N**

    2 The drone is not connected to GPS and doesn't have a map of the building.   **Y**   **N**

    3 The drone doesn't have a camera.   **Y**   **N**

    4 The drone is remotely controlled by someone.   **Y**   **N**

    5 The drone is not controlled by anyone.   **Y**   **N**

E CRITICAL THINKING

    Applying Vijay Kumar says, "Robots like this can really change the way we do K-12 education." How do you think drones could be used in K-12 education? Discuss with a partner.

VOCABULARY IN CONTEXT

A ▶ **9.12** Watch the excerpts from the TED Talk. Choose the correct meaning of the words.

B Complete the sentences with the words from the box.

figure out	jump through hoops	on the fly	team with

1 It's not easy to deliver a speech _____ ; you usually need to prepare for it.

2 You may need to _____ if you want to borrow a large sum of money from the bank.

3 If we could _____ what animals are saying, we'd be able to learn a lot more about them.

4 In my final year in college, I had to _____ a classmate to build a robot.

PRESENTATION SKILLS Referring to visuals

> If you use visuals, let the audience know when you are referring to them. There are various expressions you can use to do this. For example:
>
> *As you can see (here), …*   *Take a look at …*
>
> *Here you see/you'll see …*   *Please turn your attention to …*
>
> *Here we have …*   *If you'll look at …*

A ▶ **9.13** Watch part of Vijay Kumar's TED Talk. Complete the sentences with the expressions he uses.

1 "And _____ , _____ Daniel throw this hoop into the air, while the robot is calculating the position of the hoop, and trying to figure out how to best go through the hoop."

2 "_____ , they collapse from a three-dimensional formation into planar formation."

3 "_____ in this figure-eight flight, they come within inches of each other."

B Work with a partner. Brainstorm more phrases you could use to draw attention to visuals in a presentation.

Leafcutter ants (*Atta colombica*) in Costa Rica

 9E Thinking ahead

COMMUNICATE Debating

A Work in groups. You are going to have a debate on the topic: Should we continue to develop drone technology? **Group A:** You think drones are useful and we should continue to develop them.
Group B: You think drones are harmful. You are against developing them.

B In your group, think of at least three arguments and examples that support your position. Also, think about possible counter arguments and how you would respond. Make notes in the chart below.

Arguments supporting your position	Possible counter arguments

C Have a debate on the topic. Take turns explaining why your group's position is better.

> **Expressing disagreement**
> I don't think that's quite true.
> I'm afraid I disagree with that.
> Actually, I'd say that ...
> I see your point, but we think ...

WRITING Discussing the applications of a technology

Write a short essay. What applications of drone technology would you like to see? How would that change the way we do things?

Personally, I would like to see drones being used to help people who have difficulty getting around. Drones can help deliver groceries to them or allow them to …

A delivery drone from online shopping company Rakuten

Presentation 3

MODEL PRESENTATION

A Complete the transcript of the presentation using the words in the box.

has employed	discover	invest	will create
passionate	innovations	could	prosthetic

Hi. My name is Joel. I'm so pleased to be here. Today, I'll be discussing something that I am very [1]_____ about: space exploration.

I'm sure you've all heard of the space agency NASA. Some people claim that its space program is a waste of money. How many of you agree? Well, I personally believe it's money well spent. For one thing, many medical [2]_____ have been developed as a direct effect of space exploration. For example, when NASA was designing robots for space exploration, it developed shock-absorbing materials that are used today to help make [3]_____ limbs more comfortable.

Also, space exploration creates jobs. Since its beginnings, NASA [4]_____ thousands of engineers, scientists, and support staff. And a recent study shows that commercial space exploration [5]_____ an average of 11,800 jobs per year over the next five years.

Finally, space exploration [6]_____ help save the human race. Pretend you live in a world destroyed by global warming. Space exploration gives us the opportunity to [7]_____ new planets to live on. Even Stephen Hawking says that we may need to escape "our fragile planet" one day. We must therefore continue to [8]_____ in the space program. Thank you very much.

B ▶ **P.3** Watch the presentation and check your answers.

C ▶ **P.3** Review the list of presentation skills from Units 1–9 below. Which does the speaker use? Check (✓) them as you watch again. Then compare with a partner.

The speaker …
- ☐ asks the audience questions
- ☐ asks the audience to imagine themselves in a particular situation
- ☐ uses examples the audience is familiar with
- ☐ uses props
- ☐ begins with a strong statement
- ☐ explains technical words that the audience may not understand
- ☐ raises their hand above their head
- ☐ includes a quote

YOUR TURN

A You are going to plan and give a short presentation that argues for or against robotic surgery. Give some background information on the topic, think about what your position is, and explain your reasons. Make notes in the chart below.

> Background information (e.g. recent trends or statistics)
>
> Your position (for or against)
>
> Reasons for your position

B Look at the useful phrases in the box below. Think about which ones you will need in your presentation.

> **Useful phrases**
>
> **Stating your position:** *I'm convinced that …*
> *Personally, I believe …*
>
> **Listing points:** *For one thing, …*
> *Another reason I'm for / against …*
>
> **Giving examples:** *For instance, …*
> *As proof of that, …*

C Work with a partner. Take turns giving your presentation using your notes. Use some of the presentation skills from Units 1–9 below. As you listen, check (✓) each skill your partner uses.

> The speaker …
> ☐ asks the audience questions
> ☐ asks the audience to imagine themselves in a particular situation
> ☐ uses examples the audience is familiar with
> ☐ uses props
> ☐ begins with a strong statement
> ☐ explains technical words that the audience may not understand
> ☐ raises their hand above their head
> ☐ includes a quote

D Give your partner some feedback on their talk. Include at least two things you liked and one thing that could be improved.

10 Connections

" We spend roughly 60 percent of our communication time listening, but we're not very good at it. **"**

Julian Treasure
Author and blogger, TED speaker

UNIT GOALS

In this unit, you will ...

- talk about how to be a good listener.
- read about why we are not good at listening.
- watch a TED Talk about "conscious listening."

WARM UP

▶ **10.1** Watch part of Julian Treasure's TED Talk. Answer the questions with a partner.

1 Treasure says, "We retain just 25 percent of what we hear." Do you agree with him?

2 Do you know anyone who is a good listener? What makes them a good listener?

A group of children listen intently to a story.

10A Our listening

VOCABULARY Collocations with *listen*

A ▶ **10.2** Complete the sentences. Circle the correct words. Then listen and check your answers.

1 The students all listened (**carefully** / **sympathetically**) as the teacher explained what to do.

2 All the voters listened (**anxiously** / **politely**) as the winner of the election was announced.

3 Despite the fact that the speech was much too long, everyone listened (**patiently** / **anxiously**).

4 The children listened (**effectively** / **with great interest**) to the storyteller.

5 A good doctor should listen (**sympathetically** / **with half an ear**) to patients' complaints.

6 We are often told to respect our elders and to listen (**politely** / **reluctantly**) to what they have to say.

B Work with a partner. Take turns asking how you would listen in the following situations. Choose from the collocations in **A**, and give reasons for your choices.

1 You are at an airport and there is an announcement about a delay to your flight.

2 You are at a soccer match and the national anthem is being played.

3 A close friend is giving you relationship advice even though you didn't ask for it.

4 You are at a conference and the speaker is using technical jargon that you don't understand.

If you're at an airport and there's an announcement about a delay, how would you listen?

I'd listen really …, because …

LISTENING Mediation

A ▶ **10.3** Watch David Walker talk about the kinds of issues he deals with as a mediator. What specific example does he give? How did he resolve the dispute?

B ▶ **10.4** Watch and list three tips Walker gives to improve our listening skills.

1 _____

2 _____

3 _____

C CRITICAL THINKING

Reflecting Do you think you would be a good mediator? Why or why not? Discuss with a partner.

David Walker is an experienced mediator.

SPEAKING Staying focused

A ▶ **10.5** How does Speaker B stay focused in meetings?

A: Can I borrow your notes from today's meeting?

B: Sure. But why do you need them? Weren't you there too?

A: Yeah, but I was a bit distracted. I find it very difficult to concentrate in long meetings like that. My mind's always wandering.

B: Well, it's not always easy to stay focused. When I'm in a meeting, I find it helpful to turn my cell phone on "silent" and then put it somewhere I can't see it.

A: I tried that, but it didn't work. I still got sidetracked thinking about other things.

B: Hmm. Maybe you should join in the discussions more. Whenever I find myself getting distracted, I try to stay engaged by asking questions. You were pretty quiet in today's meeting.

A: You're right. I'll try to speak up more in tomorrow's session. Hopefully that'll help me stay focused and listen carefully.

B Practice the conversation with a partner.

C Work with a partner. How do you stay focused when listening to your teacher in class? Use the expressions in blue above to help you.

> Whenever I get distracted in class, I look at the teacher and try to make eye contact with her.

> That's a good idea. I find it helpful to …

10B Sound facts

LANGUAGE FOCUS Learning to listen

A ▶ **10.6** Read the information. Which fact do you find most surprising?

INTERESTING FACTS ABOUT SOUND

The next time you get ready to have a conversation with someone, consider these facts about sound and listening.

85% of what we learn is through listening (not talking or reading).

Less than **2%** of the population has had formal training on how to listen.

After listening to someone talk, we can immediately recall about **50%** of what was said. One hour later, we remember less than **20%** of what we heard.

We think at least **four** times faster than we speak.

In a spoken message, only **7%** is conveyed by the words used. **55%** of the meaning is derived from facial expressions, and **38%** is indicated by the tone of voice.

Words are processed by our short-term memory. **Images** go directly into long-term memory.

B ▶ **10.7** Listen to the conversation. What was Tom's problem? What does Jane suggest?

C ▶ **10.8** Watch and study the language in the chart.

Reporting what someone said		
"Listening is a learned process."	He said / told me	(that) listening was a learned process.
"You'll have to bring your notes tomorrow."	She said (that) I would have to bring my notes the next day.	
"Don't interrupt."	He told me not to interrupt.	
"How did your test go?"	She asked him how his test had gone.	
"You should use audio-visuals."	She suggested that I use audio-visuals.	
"I'll buy you lunch today."	He promised to buy her lunch that day.	
According to experts, multitasking is often a barrier to effective listening.		

For more information on **reported speech**, see Grammar Summary 10 on page 188.

D ▶ **10.7** Listen to the conversation in **B** again. Using reported speech, write what the speakers said.

1 "How did your presentation go this morning?"
She asked him _____

2 "I'll try to use more visual aids and slides tomorrow."
He said that _____

3 "Don't worry."
She told him _____

E Complete the information with the words from the box. Two options are extra.

| suggested | explained | according to | were |
| promised | called | said | are |

¹_____ Richard Branson—the founder of Virgin Group—the best

leaders ²_____ great listeners. In an interview with *Forbes*, he

³_____ why listening was important for good leadership, and shared

anecdotes from his own business dealings. He ⁴_____ that business

leaders need to listen carefully to feedback from staff and customers, which requires

effort and focus. Unfortunately, many people think of listening as a passive activity;

Branson even ⁵_____ it a "dying art." In order to improve people's active

listening, he ⁶_____ that we pay close attention not just to what someone

says, but the way in which they say it—their body language and facial expressions.

SPEAKING A survey

A Work in pairs. The graph below shows the results of a survey. Tell your partner about it. Take turns reporting each statement.

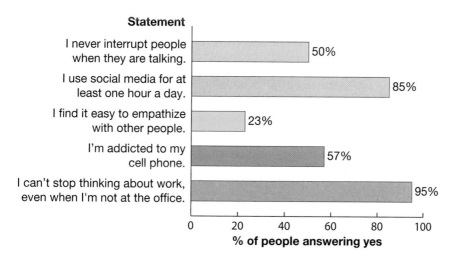

Statement

I never interrupt people when they are talking. — 50%

I use social media for at least one hour a day. — 85%

I find it easy to empathize with other people. — 23%

I'm addicted to my cell phone. — 57%

I can't stop thinking about work, even when I'm not at the office. — 95%

0   20   40   60   80   100
% of people answering yes

Fifty percent of people said that ...

According to the survey, 85 percent of people ...

B With your partner, discuss whether each statement in the graph helps or prevents effective listening. Give reasons for your conclusions.

10C The lost art of listening?

PRE-READING Predicting/Skimming

A Who do you think are generally better listeners: high school students or younger kids? Predict and discuss with a partner.

B Skim the first two paragraphs. Check your prediction.

▶ 10.9

1 Do you think you're a good listener? Chances are you do. But studies show that most people seriously **overestimate** their ability to listen. The truth is we are generally not
5 good at listening, and our listening comprehension declines as we age.

This was proven by Dr. Ralph Nichols, a **pioneer** in the scientific study of listening behavior. With the help of school teachers in Minnesota, he conducted
10 a simple experiment to test students' listening skills. He had teachers stop what they were doing mid-class, and then asked students to describe what their teachers had been talking about. You might assume that older kids, with more developed
15 brains, would be better listeners. The results, however, showed otherwise: While 90 percent of first- and second-graders gave correct responses, this percentage dropped rapidly as the students got older. A little under half of junior high students could
20 remember correctly, and only 25 percent of high school students got the answers right.

So why aren't we good at listening? One reason concerns the speed at which we think. The adult brain can process up to around 400 words per
25 minute, more than three times faster than the speed an average person speaks. This means that we can easily think about something else while someone is talking to us, allowing our mind to wander or get sidetracked. Thinking about how you will reply while
30 someone is still talking is one of the most common

barriers to effective listening. The younger students in Dr. Nichols's experiment were better listeners partly because their brains were less developed—they lacked the extra brain power to be distracted.

35 Another factor that contributes to our poor listening is our ever-decreasing attention span. According to a study conducted by Microsoft, the age of smartphones has had a negative impact here. In 2000—around the time the mobile
40 revolution began—the average human attention span was 12 seconds; by 2013, it had fallen to 8 seconds. Even a goldfish—with an average attention span of 9 seconds—can hold a thought for longer!

45 Our mobile devices also provide constant distractions, which can be very **disruptive** to listening.

Mobile devices are changing the way people interact, and can negatively affect our listening ability.

Test results have shown that being interrupted by a cell phone message (or even just expecting a message) lowers listening comprehension by 20
50 percent. Similar results were observed even before the age of digital technology. According to a 1987 study, people could remember only about 10 percent of a face-to-face conversation following a brief distraction.

Interruptions and other distractions, whether
55 digital or more traditional, can cause a dramatic decline in listening ability—but they don't have to. More and more people now realize that listening is a skill that can be developed through practice. Learning to observe a speaker's body language and emotions,
60 for example, can improve our active listening. Even the simple act of note-taking or making eye contact can help us stay focused while listening.

Many schools and businesses now provide courses in effective listening, as it has been
65 proven to **enhance** teamwork and build **rapport**. Research also suggests that people who are good listeners make better leaders. A study in the *Academy of Management Journal* indicated that employees who don't believe their bosses
70 are listening to them are less likely to offer helpful suggestions and new ideas.

The fact is that listening plays a central role in everything we do—both socially and professionally—so the rewards of effective listening
75 are many. As Dr. Ralph Nichols once said, "The most basic of all human needs is the need to understand and be understood. The best way to understand people is to listen to them."

UNDERSTANDING MAIN IDEAS

Which sentence is the author most likely to agree with?

a There are many techniques we can use to help us stay focused while listening, but the best way to improve our listening skills is to limit our use of modern technology.

b Effective listening is something we all do automatically, although most of us need to be taught the proper tools and techniques in order to be good at it.

c The mobile revolution has had a negative impact on our ability to listen, but there are various techniques we can use to improve our listening skills.

IDENTIFYING CAUSE AND EFFECT

Complete the diagram showing causes and effects.

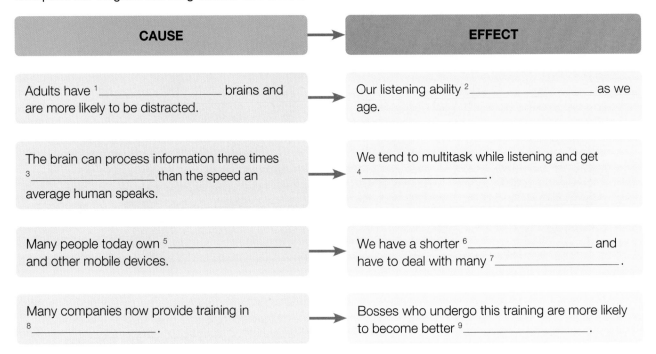

CAUSE	EFFECT
Adults have [1]_____ brains and are more likely to be distracted.	Our listening ability [2]_____ as we age.
The brain can process information three times [3]_____ than the speed an average human speaks.	We tend to multitask while listening and get [4]_____ .
Many people today own [5]_____ and other mobile devices.	We have a shorter [6]_____ and have to deal with many [7]_____ .
Many companies now provide training in [8]_____ .	Bosses who undergo this training are more likely to become better [9]_____ .

BUILDING VOCABULARY

A Match the words in blue from the passage to their definitions.

1 overestimate ○   ○ one who is first or among the earliest to do something

2 pioneer ○   ○ to make something better; improve

3 disruptive ○   ○ a good relationship or understanding among a group of people

4 enhance ○   ○ to judge too highly or favorably

5 rapport ○   ○ causing trouble and therefore stopping an activity from continuing as usual

B CRITICAL THINKING

Reflecting What behavior mentioned in the passage are you most guilty of? What can you do to change this? Discuss with a partner.

10D Five ways to listen better

TEDTALKS

JULIAN TREASURE is an expert on sound and communication. He focuses on how we can listen in a more **conscious** way to enhance communication. This involves **savoring** different kinds of sounds—from the **mundane** and **trivial**, to the unusual and **subtle**.

Julian Treasure's idea worth spreading is that in a fast-paced world where everyone is competing for attention, "conscious listening" may be the only way we can truly understand one another and maintain meaningful relationships.

PREVIEWING

Read the paragraphs above. Match each **bold** word to its meaning. You will hear these words in the TED Talk.

1 everyday; normal   _____

2 enjoying   _____

3 having qualities not easy to notice   _____

4 not important   _____

5 aware of one's surroundings and knowing what is happening   _____

VIEWING

A ▶ **10.10** Read the scenarios below. Then watch Part 1 of the TED Talk. Match the listening techniques in the box to the correct scenario. Write **a**, **b**, or **c**.

a pattern recognition	**b** differencing	**c** filtering

Scenario 1
You move from the countryside to the city. At first, you find it hard to sleep because of all the traffic and general noise. After a few weeks, you get used to it and hardly notice the noise.

Scenario 2
You are listening to a lecture. You are only interested in some key facts and figures. You are not paying attention to anything else the speaker is saying.

Scenario 3
You are at a party, surrounded by lots of people talking. A friend arrives and calls out your name. You hear him, even though it is noisy and he is several meters away.

Listening technique: _____

Listening technique: _____

Listening technique: _____

B ▶ **10.11** Watch Part 2 of the TED Talk. Would Julian Treasure agree with the following statements? Circle **Y** for yes or **N** for no.

1 Sounds help define our surroundings.   **Y**   **N**

2 Listening is difficult and tiring because the world is now so noisy.   **Y**   **N**

3 Many people nowadays prefer quick sound bites to actual conversations.   **Y**   **N**

4 We are becoming more sensitive to noise and what's being said in the media.   **Y**   **N**

5 It's less important for us to practice conscious listening now because of   **Y**   **N**
    modern technology.

C ▶ **10.12** Watch Part 3 of the TED Talk. Match each tool for conscious listening in the box to its corresponding exercise.

silence	the mixer	savoring

1 Listen closely to the ticking of a clock. Nod your head in time with the "beat" of the clock, as if you are listening to music on headphones.
    Tool: _____

2 Find a quiet area in your house, and sit on the floor in a cross-legged position. Close your eyes, clear your mind, and meditate for a few minutes.
    Tool: _____

3 Listen to a song and identify the different instruments and voices you hear. Practice differentiating one sound from another.
    Tool: _____

D ▶ **10.12** Watch Part 3 of the TED Talk again. What does the acronym RASA mean? Fill out the acronym in the space provided on the right.

(R) _____

(A) _____

(S) _____

(A) _____

E CRITICAL THINKING

Applying Which statement below do you personally agree with the most? Explain your reasoning to a partner and give examples. As you discuss, take turns applying the RASA techniques.

a I want to make a list of mundane sounds and practice savoring each of them.

b I think conscious listening is an important skill and should be taught in schools.

c I need to limit my use of social media and have more meaningful face-to-face conversations with my friends.

VOCABULARY IN CONTEXT

▶ **10.13** Watch the excerpts from the TED Talk. Choose the correct meaning of the words.

PRESENTATION SKILLS Using acronyms to summarize

Using acronyms is an effective way to help your audience remember and understand key points or steps. To form an acronym, take the first letter of each word you are trying to remember. Next, arrange the letters into a word that is easy to pronounce. You can add vowels if necessary.

When using an acronym for the first time in a presentation, make sure you explain its meaning properly.

A ▶ **10.14** Watch part of Julian Treasure's TED Talk. How does he introduce the acronym RASA and explain its meaning? Complete the excerpt below with the phrase he uses.

"And finally, an acronym … the acronym is RASA, which is the Sanskrit word for juice or essence. And RASA _____ *Receive*, which means pay attention to the person; *Appreciate*, making little noises like 'hmm,' 'oh,' 'OK'; *Summarize*, the word 'so' is very important in communication; and *Ask*, ask questions afterwards."

B Below are two common acronyms. Fill out each of them in the space provided. You may look them up if you're not sure what they mean.

(N) _____   (P) _____

(A) _____   (O) _____

(S) _____   (T) _____

(A) _____   (U) _____

                                                         (S) _____

C Work with a partner. What other acronyms can you think of? What do they mean?

10E Conscious listening

COMMUNICATE How good are your listening skills?

A Are you a good listener? Read the questions below and check (✓) your answers.

When someone is talking to you, do you ...	Not usually	Sometimes	Yes, I usually do
1 keep an eye on the clock?	☐	☐	☐
2 make eye contact with the speaker?	☐	☐	☐
3 pay attention to the speaker's body language?	☐	☐	☐
4 check your cell phone for messages as you listen?	☐	☐	☐
5 interrupt the speaker if they say something you disagree with?	☐	☐	☐
6 think about how you'll reply as you listen?	☐	☐	☐
7 listen more for facts than for feelings?	☐	☐	☐
8 take notes about important information you've heard?	☐	☐	☐
9 wait for the speaker to finish before forming an opinion?	☐	☐	☐
10 make physical gestures (like nodding) to show that you're listening?	☐	☐	☐

B Work with a partner. Take turns asking and answering the questions. Circle your partner's answers.

C Look back at the answers. With your partner, discuss whether you are each good at conscious listening, and give reasons for your conclusions. You may ask follow-up questions to get more information if necessary.

> I think I'm a good listener because I ...

> That's true. But you also sometimes ...

Asking follow-up questions
Can you elaborate on that, please?   *Can you give an example?*

WRITING A survey report

Look at the results above. Write one or two paragraphs summarizing the results of the survey, and include details about what makes a good listener.

> The survey showed that while I'm generally a pretty good listener, there are still some things I can work on to improve my listening skills. In particular, I tend to keep an eye on the clock during conversations. This is a bad habit because ...
>
> According to the survey, David is good at conscious listening because ...

11 Life in the Slow Lane

" [Cloudspotting] is a pointless activity, which is precisely why it's so important. "

Gavin Pretor-Pinney
Science writer, TED speaker

UNIT GOALS

In this unit, you will ...

- talk about slowing down and monotasking.
- read about how nature affects the brain.
- watch a TED Talk about clouds and how we can benefit from appreciating them.

WARM UP

▶ **11.1** Watch part of Gavin Pretor-Pinney's TED Talk. Answer the questions with a partner.

1 Did you enjoy looking up at the clouds when you were a child? Why or why not?

2 Can you think of any English expressions that mention clouds? Are these expressions positive or negative?

A cheese stand at a Slow Food event in Turin, Italy

11A The slow movement

VOCABULARY Slowing down

A Read the paragraph below. Then match each **bold** word to its definition.

Today, people are living increasingly stressful lives trying to **juggle** work, family, and friends. There never seems to be enough time to do everything. As a result, many of us feel a need to rush through life. We now have faster cars, faster Internet, even "fast food." In response to the rush of modern life, a growing number of people have embraced the "Slow Movement." This began in 1986, when Carlo Petrini founded Slow Food to protest against the opening of the first McDonald's in Italy. He wanted to **restore** an **appreciation** for local food cultures and traditions, and promote quality over convenience. The Slow Movement encourages us to do things like eating and exercising in a more **leisurely** way, and to be more aware of our surroundings. This way, we can develop more **meaningful** ties with other people.

1 juggle	○	○ relaxed; without hurry
2 restore	○	○ to balance or keep several activities in progress
3 appreciation	○	○ to bring back
4 leisurely	○	○ assessment of the true value of something
5 meaningful	○	○ worthwhile; significant

B Cross out the word that does NOT collocate with each **bold** word.

1 **juggle**	projects	responsibilities	~~experiences~~	jobs
2 **restore**	balance	effort	order	confidence
3 **leisurely**	walk	meal	pace	hotel
4 **meaningful**	conversation	expert	relationship	life

C Work with a partner. Below are some branches of the Slow Movement. What kinds of activities do you think each one does?

| Slow Exercise | Slow Reading | Slow Travel | Slow Fashion |

LISTENING Living in the present

> **Repeating main ideas**
> Speakers sometimes repeat key points from their talk for emphasis or to make their main ideas clearer.
>
> *Again, ...*   *Like I said before, ...*   *As mentioned earlier, ...*

A ▶ **11.2** Watch author Carl Honoré talk about the importance of slowing down. Who helped him realize he was living life too fast?

B ▶ **11.2** Watch again. What is Honoré's main message?

  a By doing things slowly, we can make sure we do them correctly.

  b We need to do things at the right speed for ourselves—faster isn't always better.

  c Leading a slower-paced life gives us more freedom to explore and try new things.

C **CRITICAL THINKING**

  Reflecting Are there aspects of your own life you would like to slow down? Discuss with a partner.

Carl Honoré, author of the best-selling book *In Praise of Slowness*

SPEAKING Leading a slower-paced life

A ▶ **11.3** How will the camping retreat help Speaker A unwind?

  A: It's Friday. Finally!

  B: Yeah, it's been a long week. Do you have any plans for the weekend?

  A: I'm going on a camping retreat with David.

  B: Oh, that's right. He was telling me about it. It's the one where you aren't allowed to bring your cell phones or laptops, right?

  A: Yeah. I'm really looking forward to it. Things at work have been so hectic lately that I've barely had time to sleep. I seriously need to get away from work for a while.

  B: What kind of activities will you be doing there?

  A: Hiking mostly, maybe some kayaking. And we'll probably do a bit of yoga as well. It'll be good to slow down and take things easy for a change.

  B: I've never been to a retreat before, but I've always found that hiking makes me feel happier. It's a great way to unwind. You're going to have a great weekend.

B Practice the conversation with a partner.

C Work with a partner. Talk about how you could slow down and enjoy life more. Use the expressions in blue above to help you.

> I think that cycling instead of driving is a great way to slow down and unwind.

> I'd like to go on vacation to a remote village in the countryside because ...

11B Time to monotask

LANGUAGE FOCUS Multitasking versus monotasking

A ▶ **11.4** Read the information. Do you think you are a true multitasker?

THE TRUTH ABOUT **MULTITASKING**

People who multitask might feel like they're accomplishing more, but they're actually getting less done in the process.

Our brains are designed to focus on **one** thing at a time. When people think they're multitasking, they're really only changing from one task to another very rapidly.

People who think they're the best at multitasking are almost always **the worst**.

Just knowing about an unread email or message can keep us distracted and reduce a person's effective IQ by **10 points**.

Listening to a cell phone while driving can reduce a driver's concentration by about **37%**.

Multitasking **reduces** the efficiency and quality of our work. Each time we switch tasks, it takes time and effort to refocus.

Only about **2%** of the population are true multitaskers. These people can multitask without losing efficiency or quality.

B ▶ **11.5** Listen to the conversation. Why was Nicholas distracted while driving? What is Sarah's advice?

C ▶ **11.6** Watch and study the language in the chart.

Talking about quantity
Articles: *a*, *an*, *the*, zero article
Multitasking takes a toll on the brain.
Experts say that social media can become an addiction.
A new poll shows that the average U.S. employee spends 6.3 hours checking email every day.
Young people often prefer texting to talking on the phone.
Quantifiers
Every time we switch tasks, the brain uses a little bit of energy to refocus.
Information overload can cause a lot of stress over time.
It's important to prioritize when you have to juggle a large number of projects.
A huge amount of data flows through the Internet each second.

For more information on **articles and quantifiers**, see Grammar Summary 11 on page 189.

D ▶ `11.5` Listen to the conversation in **B** again. Complete the sentences from the conversation.

1 "I had to stop _____ car _____ times to check _____ directions."

2 "No, _____ address was correct. It was my fault. I had to take _____ work call while I was driving."

3 "_____ accidents happen because people try to multitask while driving."

E ▶ `11.7` Complete the information. Circle the correct words. If no article is necessary, circle **x**. Then listen and check your answers.

Earl Miller is ¹(**the** / **a**) famous scientist and ²(**the** / **an**) expert on multitasking and ³(**the** / **x**) brain. He says that ⁴(**a** / **x**) multitasking can be addictive because every time we complete a small task—like sending ⁵(**an** / **the**) email or answering ⁶(**a** / **the**) text message—the brain releases ⁷(**x** / **the**) pleasure chemical dopamine. Over time, however, this constant task-switching leads to anxiety and stress. In fact, multitasking has been found to increase production of ⁸(**x** / **the**) stress hormone cortisol in the brain, which can lead to health problems like diabetes, heart disease, and even ⁹(**a** / **x**) depression.

Earl Miller, brain expert

F Complete the sentences with the words from the box. One option is extra.

each	very few	too much	many	a little bit of

1 Employees can become overwhelmed and make mistakes when they have to deal with _____ information.

2 _____ people are truly able to multitask.

3 _____ people now believe that multitasking is a bad habit.

4 We should stop multitasking and instead, do _____ task separately.

SPEAKING A multitasking test

A Work in pairs. Take turns doing the following tasks, and time yourselves. Compare your results with your partner. What do you find?

1 On a separate piece of paper, write your full name. As you do so, spell aloud the sentence, "I am multitasking."

2 On a separate piece of paper, write your full name. As soon as you are finished, spell aloud the sentence, "I am multitasking."

B Share your results with the class. Are they similar? How many students performed faster when multitasking? What does this suggest?

I was quicker when I did the two tasks separately.

I made more mistakes when I …

11C Your brain on nature

PRE-READING Predicting

Look at the photo. How do you think the man in the photo is feeling? How do you feel when you are surrounded by nature?

▶ 11.8

1 After a morning hike in the Saneum Healing Forest east of Seoul, 46-year-old firefighter Kang Byoung-wook sips tea made from the bark of an elm tree, practices yoga, enjoys an
5 arm massage, and makes a collage from dried flowers. He is one of about 40 firefighters taking part in a three-day program sponsored by the local government. The aim of the program is to offer "forest healing"; the firefighters all have post-
10 traumatic stress disorder.

Saneum is one of three official healing forests in South Korea, which offer a range of programs from meditation to woodcraft to camping. Soon there will be 34 more. South Koreans—many of
15 whom suffer from work stress, digital **addiction**, and intense academic pressures—have embraced the medicalization of nature with great enthusiasm. In fact, Korea's Chungbuk University offers a "forest healing" degree program, and the government
20 is investing a hundred million dollars in a healing complex next to Sobaeksan National Park.

There is increasing evidence that being outside in a pleasant natural environment is good for us. But how many of us get to enjoy nature regularly? Fewer
25 and fewer, it seems. According to Lisa Nisbet, a psychology professor at Canada's Trent University, evidence for the benefits of nature is pouring in at a time when we are most disconnected from it. The pressures of modern life lead to long hours
30 spent working indoors. Digital addiction and strong academic pressure add to the problem. In America, visits to parks have been declining since the

dawn of email, and so have visits to the backyard. Research indicates that only about 10 percent of
35 American teens spend time outside every day. "We don't think of [being outdoors] as a way to increase happiness," says Nisbet. "We think other things will, like shopping or TV." But some countries, like South Korea, are starting to challenge this mindset.

40 So what are some of the benefits of nature that Nisbet refers to? Being surrounded by nature has one obvious effect: It calms us and reduces our stress levels. This has been shown to lower blood pressure, heart rates, and levels of the
45 stress hormone cortisol, as well as reduce feelings of fear or anger. But studies also indicate that spending time in nature can do more than provide an improved sense of well-being; it can lower rates of heart disease, asthma, and diabetes. This is
50 probably because we **evolved** in nature and are adapted to understanding its signs.

A hiker in Washington State's
Olympic National Park

Spending time outdoors also makes us happier and can lead to a boost of energy—a sense of being more alive. Just 20 minutes a day in nature
55 is enough to make a significant difference. "Nature is fuel for the soul," says psychology professor Richard Ryan.

Another experiment conducted by psychologist Stephen Kaplan and his colleagues
60 found that people who took a 50-minute walk in a park had better attention and short-term memory than those who took a walk along a city street. "Imagine a **therapy** that had no known side effects, was readily available, and could
65 improve your **cognitive** functioning at zero cost," the researchers wrote in their paper. It exists, they continued, and it's called "interacting with nature."

Perhaps what's more surprising is that nature
70 may also make us more creative. David Strayer, a cognitive psychologist at the University of Utah, demonstrated as much with a group of participants, who performed 50 percent better on creative problem-solving tasks after
75 three days of wilderness backpacking. When we slow down, stop the busywork, and take in beautiful natural surroundings, he says, not only do we feel restored, but our mental performance improves too.

80 We all **intuitively** know that nature is good for us. Now we are beginning to understand the many ways it benefits us and just what effects it has on the mind and body. According to Strayer, we may never know exactly what nature does to the brain.
85 Something mysterious will always remain, and maybe that's as it should be. "At the end of the day," he says, "we come out in nature not because the science says it does something to us, but because of how it makes us feel."

UNDERSTANDING MAIN IDEAS

Choose the best alternative title for the passage.

a South Korea's Natural Wonders

b The Power of Nature

c Getting Closer to Nature

UNDERSTANDING DETAILS

Which of the following does the passage mention? Check (✓) your answers.

☐ We need to take better care of the natural environment, particularly our forests and national parks.

☐ Outdoor activities like hiking and camping are useful for treating stress and attention disorders.

☐ "Forest healing" is offered as a university course in South Korea.

☐ Pollution is one of the reasons fewer and fewer Americans are spending time outdoors.

☐ Teenagers are less likely to spend time outside than adults.

☐ Spending time outdoors has both a calming and an energizing effect on us.

☐ Being in nature enhances our short-term memory and problem-solving abilities.

☐ Government officials should do more to increase people's access to nature.

BUILDING VOCABULARY

A Match the words in blue from the passage to their definitions.

1 addiction ○   ○ concerned with the act or process of thinking

2 evolved ○   ○ knowing or understanding something based on feelings rather than facts or proof

3 therapy ○   ○ developed gradually

4 cognitive ○   ○ the treatment of an illness or injury, whether physical or mental

5 intuitively ○   ○ a condition that results when a person's need to regularly do something interferes with ordinary life responsibilities

B Complete the sentences using the words in **A**.

1 Her company has _____ from a hobby into a thriving business.

2 A key contributing factor to today's fast-paced lifestyle is people's _____ to technology.

3 Language and memory are examples of basic _____ abilities.

4 Contact with nature is increasingly used as a form of _____ by mental health professionals.

5 Some entrepreneurs prefer to make decisions _____ instead of relying on data or asking other people for advice.

C CRITICAL THINKING

Analyzing What things could you do to spend more time outdoors in nature? What could the government do to help? Discuss with a partner.

11D Cloudy with a chance of joy

TEDTALKS

GAVIN PRETOR-PINNEY is a science writer. His writing combines science with an appreciation of the natural wonders around us. He co-founded *The Idler* magazine, a publication that encourages people to take time out of their busy routines to enjoy their surroundings. He also founded the Cloud Appreciation Society, an organization devoted to the idle pursuit of cloud watching.

Gavin Pretor-Pinney's idea worth spreading is that we can all benefit from looking up and admiring the beauty of the clouds over our heads.

PREVIEWING

Read the sentences. Choose the option that has a similar meaning to each **bold** word. You will hear these words in the TED Talk.

1 Extreme weather events like hurricanes can cause fallen trees and road **obstructions**.

   a obstacles   **b** signs

2 Most explorers have a **fondness** for the natural world.

   a ambition   **b** affection

3 **Meditation** is a good way to relax and relieve stress.

   a quiet thought   **b** nervousness

4 You've got to **stand up for** what you believe in.

   a defend   **b** dismiss

5 Some common things people **moan** about are heavy traffic, bad weather, and slow Wi-Fi.

   a care   **b** complain

VIEWING

A ▶ **11.9** Watch Part 1 of the TED Talk. Would Gavin Pretor-Pinney agree with the following statements? Circle **Y** for yes or **N** for no.

1 A lot of people don't notice how beautiful clouds really are.   **Y**   **N**

2 Clouds are annoying because they block the sun.   **Y**   **N**

3 Clouds can stimulate our imagination.   **Y**   **N**

4 Cloud watching is more fun when you're young.   **Y**   **N**

5 How we think or feel can influence what shapes we see in the clouds.   **Y**   **N**

B ▶ **11.10** Watch Part 2 of the TED Talk. Match the clouds (**1–4**) to the pictures.

1 cirrus
2 lenticularis

3 fallstreak holes
4 Kelvin-Helmholtz

a

b

c

d

C Match the types of clouds to their descriptions.

1 cirrus ○

2 lenticularis ○

3 fallstreak holes ○

4 Kelvin-Helmholtz ○

○ formed when the wind rises to pass over mountains

○ formed when water droplets in the cloud start to freeze into ice crystals

○ caused by different wind speeds above and below the cloud layer

○ high up; made of ice crystals that are blown by strong winds

D ▶ **11.11** Watch Part 3 of the TED Talk. Check (✓) the statements that Gavin Pretor-Pinney would agree with.

☐ The cumulonimbus storm cloud is the best cloud for finding shapes in.

☐ Cloudspotting on a sunny day is a waste of time.

☐ Cloudspotting is important because there's no real point in doing it.

☐ Feeling that you're in the present moment is beneficial in many ways.

E CRITICAL THINKING

Synthesizing Compare Gavin Pretor-Pinney's recommendations with the advice given by Julian Treasure in Unit 10. How are they similar? Discuss with a partner.

VOCABULARY IN CONTEXT

▶ **11.12** Watch the excerpts from the TED Talk. Choose the correct meaning of the words.

PRESENTATION SKILLS Being enthusiastic

It's important to be enthusiastic about your topic. Your audience will become more involved and will pay more attention to what you're saying. You can show your enthusiasm by:

• varying the speed and volume of your delivery;

• using facial expressions and body language that convey the interest you feel in the topic;

• using questions and gestures to invite the audience to share your enthusiasm;

• using visuals that show what there is to enjoy about your topic.

A ▶ **11.13** Watch part of Gavin Pretor-Pinney's TED Talk. Which of the techniques above does he use?

B Choose a topic you know a lot about or an activity you enjoy doing. It could be a place, a sport, or a hobby. Make brief notes on three things you want to communicate about your topic, and practice your presentation. Try to use at least one of the techniques in the Tip box.

C Work in small groups. Take turns giving your presentations. Note the ways your group members show their enthusiasm.

Mick Ohrberg (Member 14,198)
Kansas City, Missouri, US

149

Changing the pace

COMMUNICATE Slow movement organizations

A Work in small groups. You are going to create an organization that encourages people to slow down, appreciate simple things, and live more in the present. It could focus on nature, food, travel, or your own idea. Make notes in the chart below.

Name of organization	Area of focus	Activities or programs offered

B As a group, tell the class about your organization and how it helps people enjoy life more. Invite your classmates to ask follow-up questions.

> **Handling questions**
> *Thank you for asking. We plan to …*   *That's a great question. Our strategy is to …*

C Which organization would you like to join? Hold a class vote.

WRITING An advertisement

Choose either your own organization or one of the other organizations you heard about above, and write an advertisement for it. Explain what the organization does and how it will benefit people.

> Fancy a surfing vacation? Tired of the usual "touristy" beaches? Look no further. At Surf Spot, we help surfers avoid all the usual tourist traps of a beach vacation, and instead, put more emphasis on the local communities and culture. We can help you …

Sedgefield, South Africa—a member of the Slow Town movement—attracts many surfers.

12 Make Yourself Heard

" So how do organizations think? Well, for the most part, they don't ... because the people inside of them are too afraid of conflict. "

Margaret Heffernan
Management thinker, TED speaker

UNIT GOALS

In this unit, you will ...

- talk about people who had the courage to express their views.
- read about famous whistleblowers.
- watch a TED Talk about the importance of challenging accepted wisdom.

WARM UP

▶ 12.1 Watch part of Margaret Heffernan's TED Talk. Answer the questions with a partner.

1 Why do you think the executives were afraid to raise their issues or concerns?

2 How do you usually react when you disagree with someone? Do you keep quiet or voice your opinion?

Pakistani student Malala Yousafzai speaks before the United Nations Youth Assembly.

MALALA YOUSAFZAI

PRESIDENT OF THE GENERAL ASSEMBLY

ASHWINT ANGA

12A Expressing yourself

VOCABULARY Voicing an opinion

A ▶ 12.2 Complete the sentences using the correct form of the words from the box. Then listen and check your answers.

clarify	persuade	conflict	assert	resolve

1 Despite the evidence against him, he has continued to _____ his innocence.

2 The company's problems were finally _____ when the unpopular CEO resigned.

3 The politician was asked to _____ his position on the recent tax cuts.

4 In order to avoid _____, he decided to keep his opinion to himself.

5 It can sometimes be hard to _____ people to do the right thing.

B Complete the sentences. Circle the correct words.

1 Mediators help to (**assert** / **resolve**) family disputes.

2 Both countries were hoping for a peaceful (**conflict** / **resolution**) to the crisis.

3 During court cases, lawyers often appeal to the jury's emotions in order to make their arguments more (**persuasive** / **assertive**).

C Work with a partner. Look at the picture of Malala above. What do you know about her?

LISTENING The *Challenger* disaster

> ### Listening for stressed words
> Not every word in a sentence is stressed in spoken English. We tend to stress "information" words, such as nouns, verbs, adjectives, and adverbs. Grammatical words—like prepositions, auxiliaries, and articles—tend not to be stressed.

A ▶ **12.3** Watch a description of the space shuttle *Challenger* disaster. How was NASA involved?

   a NASA made decisions based on incorrect data.

   b NASA ignored critical data.

B ▶ **12.3** Watch again. Check (✓) the effects that whistleblowing had on Roger Boisjoly.

   ☐ He became isolated and lonely.

   ☐ His health deteriorated.

   ☐ He was immediately fired from his job.

C CRITICAL THINKING

   Analyzing What does the *Challenger* disaster suggest about the organizational culture in NASA at the time? Discuss with a partner.

The final launch of the space shuttle *Challenger*

SPEAKING Standing up for your beliefs

A ▶ **12.4** What did Susan B. Anthony do?

   A: Have you decided who to write about for your social studies assignment?

   B: Yeah. I'm writing about Susan B. Anthony.

   A: I don't think I've heard of her before.

   B: She was an American civil rights leader in the early twentieth century who asserted that women should have equal rights to men. She stood up for her beliefs and fought for women's right to vote.

   A: Wow, she must have been very courageous.

   B: She was. She also called for equal educational opportunities for boys and girls. In 1900, she finally persuaded the University of Rochester to admit women.

   A: Did she ever come into conflict with the authorities for her beliefs?

   B: Yes, she did. She was arrested for voting in 1872. But she didn't let that stop her. She devoted the rest of her life to fighting for women's rights.

B Practice the conversation with a partner.

C Work with a partner. Talk about other famous people who have stood up for their beliefs. Use the expressions in blue above to help you.

> Can you think of someone famous who stood up for their beliefs?

> Malala Yousafzai. She fights for …

12B Disasters

LANGUAGE FOCUS Disasters that could have been prevented

A ▶ **12.5** Read the information. Do you know about any other famous disasters? What happened? What caused them?

PREVENTABLE DISASTERS

Throughout history, there have been many disasters that could have been avoided. Here are a few examples.

1912
TITANIC DISASTER

R.M.S. *Titanic* sank after hitting an iceberg. The crew had received multiple **iceberg warnings** and were advised to slow down, but didn't. Also, the ship had only enough lifeboats to save about half the people on board. Many lifeboats were lowered before they were full.

Casualties: over 1,500 people killed

1986
CHALLENGER DISASTER

The space shuttle *Challenger* exploded after an O-ring seal failed at lift-off. The O-ring was not designed to fly under unusually cold conditions, as in this launch. Engineers had pleaded with NASA to **postpone the launch**, but NASA rejected their advice.

Casualties: all seven crew members killed

2007
MINNEAPOLIS BRIDGE COLLAPSE

The I-35W Mississippi River Bridge collapsed suddenly in 2007. For nearly two decades before the collapse, U.S. government officials knew the bridge was "**structurally deficient**." But instead of replacing it, they relied on "patchwork repairs."

Casualties: 13 people killed, 145 others injured

B ▶ **12.6** Listen to the conversation. What caused the sinking of *Titanic*?

C ▶ **12.7** Watch and study the language in the chart.

Talking about the imaginary past

If the captain of *Titanic* had taken the ice warnings seriously, the ship probably would have missed the iceberg.

If the crew of *Titanic* had been trained properly in evacuation procedures, more people would have survived.

If the engineers employed by NASA hadn't provided critical information to investigators, we wouldn't have found out the truth about the *Challenger* disaster.

If government officials had carried out sufficient repairs on the Mississippi River Bridge, it might still be standing today.

If the Internet hadn't been invented, we wouldn't have access to so much information.

For more information on **third conditional** and **mixed conditionals**, see Grammar Summary 12 on page 190.

D ▶ **12.6** Listen to the conversation in **B** again. Complete the sentences from the conversation.

1 "If the ship _____ slower, it probably _____ time to avoid the iceberg."

2 "If there _____ the right number of lifeboats, more people _____."

3 "If the captain _____ all the necessary precautions, we probably _____ still
_____ talking about *Titanic* today."

E **Read the information. Then complete the sentences below using the correct form of the words in parentheses.**

Fires were common in London in the 17th century. Most buildings were made of wood and were very close together, so they caught fire easily. King Charles II had even warned the mayor of London about the dangers of a major fire. After a particularly hot and dry summer in September 1666, a fire broke out in a tiny bakery on Pudding Lane. The fire quickly got out of control, as a strong wind that day caused it to spread rapidly. The fire—now known as the Great Fire of London—continued to burn for four days. By the time it was over, it had destroyed 80 percent of the city and over 13,000 buildings. Luckily, only a few people died. The fire did have one positive effect, however: It killed thousands of rats that had carried the plague, and helped stop the spread of the deadly disease.

An illustration of the Great Fire of London

1 If the buildings _____ (**be**) made of wood, they wouldn't have burned so easily.

2 If the mayor of London _____ (**take**) the king's warning seriously, the fire probably wouldn't have been so bad.

3 If there hadn't been a strong wind that day, the fire _____ (**have**) spread so rapidly.

4 If there hadn't been a fire, the rats carrying the plague _____ (**have**) continued to spread the disease.

SPEAKING A moral dilemma

Work with a partner. Read the information about a fictitious disaster. Then discuss your answers to the questions below.

In order to cut costs, a toy factory used cheap materials in its production process. A few assembly line workers knew about the dangers but were too afraid to speak up. As a result, several children were harmed while playing with the toy products, and the company is being sued by the children's families.

1 How could the disaster have been prevented?

If the toy factory hadn't used cheap materials, no children would have been harmed.

If the assembly line workers had informed the media beforehand, the public would have known ...

2 What would you have done if you were one of the assembly line workers? Why?

12C Whistleblowers

Do you know of any famous whistleblowers? What is your opinion of them?

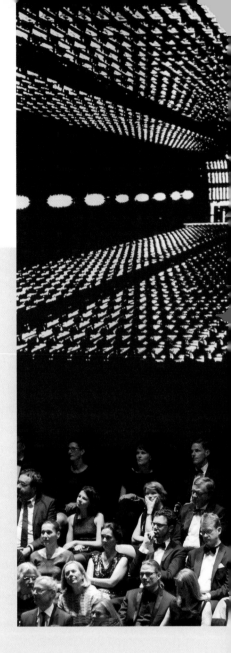

▶ 12.8

1 In late 2014, an **anonymous** source contacted a German newspaper. The source offered access to millions of internal documents from the secretive Panama law firm Mossack Fonseca.
5 Over the following year, the whistleblower leaked an **unprecedented** number of documents. The amount was so huge—over 11 million documents—that the newspaper coordinated with the International Consortium of Investigative Journalists (ICIJ) to
10 distribute the documents to around 100 media organizations in 80 countries. It took journalists over a year to analyze all this data, now known as the Panama Papers.

  The Panama Papers reveal how the rich and
15 famous—including important politicians, well-known athletes, business tycoons, and even criminals— avoided paying taxes by using complicated offshore arrangements to hide their wealth. This was one of the biggest leaks in journalistic history, but it almost certainly
20 won't be the last. Statistics from the U.S. Securities and Exchange Commission show that from 2012 to 2015, the number of whistleblower tips it received grew by more than 30 percent. As technological advances make it increasingly easy for people to share files, we
25 can expect this trend to continue. So what motivates whistleblowers? And is what they do positive?

  While some whistleblowers may be driven by revenge or self-enrichment, others may be dedicated individuals who want to make positive
30 changes to their organizations or bring **wrongdoing** to light. In 1996, Jeffrey Wigand—an employee of Brown & Williamson, an American cigarette company—exposed the tobacco industry's lies about the dangers of smoking. He revealed that
35 tobacco companies were intentionally increasing the amount of nicotine in cigarettes, despite knowing that it was highly addictive and could cause cancer. Few would argue now that what Wigand did was a bad thing. But what about revealing
40 government secrets? Does the public have a right to know everything? Or should we trust that our governments know what they're doing?

  Edward Snowden is probably the most famous whistleblower in recent years. While working for the
45 CIA and National Security Agency (NSA), he was shocked to discover how extensive the government's reach was in terms of domestic surveillance of civilians. He regarded these practices as an invasion of privacy and an abuse of power. In 2013, he leaked
50 thousands of **classified** documents from the NSA's

Edward Snowden speaks via video to an audience in Hamburg, Germany.

surveillance program to journalists, after which he was charged by the U.S. government with violating the Espionage Act. He then fled to Russia to avoid arrest. His actions have fueled much discussion
55 about the balance between information privacy and national security.

Whistleblowers often pay a high price for their actions, as organizations may **retaliate** or try to **discredit** them. Wigand received anonymous death
60 threats and required round-the-clock bodyguards. His wife divorced him, and their two daughters went to live with her. Eventually, he moved to a new city to make a fresh start. As for Snowden, he was forced to leave the country altogether. American intelligence officials
65 have stated that by releasing classified information, Snowden has damaged national security and put people's lives in danger: especially military troops and secret agents. Many people therefore view him as a criminal or a traitor who betrayed his own country. But
70 there are others who see him as a hero for standing up for freedom of speech and information.

Clearly, the consequences of whistleblowing can be very difficult to live with. This helps explain why many whistleblowers—including the source of
75 the Panama Papers—prefer to remain anonymous. There are many motivations that lie at the heart of whistleblowing, and our reactions to whistleblowers vary. In situations related to public health and safety, exposing wrongdoing seems hard to criticize.
80 However, when it comes to revealing government secrets, blowing the whistle is a much more complex issue that raises many ethical and moral questions.

UNDERSTANDING MAIN IDEAS

The main purpose of the passage is to _____.

    a explain why it is wrong for whistleblowers to do what they do

    b discuss the complexities of whistleblowing

    c present personal stories about the experiences of whistleblowers

UNDERSTANDING DETAILS

Check (✓) the statements that the author would agree with.

☐ Whistleblowers generally do more harm than good.

☐ Whistleblowing cases are likely to decrease in the future.

☐ Jeffrey Wigand is an example of a whistleblower who did the right thing.

☐ Edward Snowden broke the law, but he had good intentions behind his actions.

☐ Some cases of whistleblowing are easier to justify than others.

BUILDING VOCABULARY

A Match the words in blue from the passage to their definitions.

1 anonymous ○	○	illegal or dishonest behavior
2 unprecedented ○	○	to damage someone's reputation
3 wrongdoing ○	○	not identified by name
4 classified ○	○	having no previous example
5 retaliate ○	○	to attack or injure someone as a response to a hurtful action
6 discredit ○	○	officially secret and available only to authorized people

B Complete the sentences using the correct form of the words in **A**.

    1 There are a number of cases where organizations have _____ against whistleblowers.

    2 Releasing _____ documents is against the law.

    3 Many whistleblowers prefer to stay _____ out of fear for their safety.

    4 Companies sometimes try to _____ whistleblowers by making them appear untrustworthy.

    5 A cover-up is an attempt to hide evidence of _____.

    6 One whistleblower, Bradley Birkenfeld, received a(n) _____ reward of $104 million from the U.S. government.

C **CRITICAL THINKING**

Reflecting If you were able to interview Edward Snowden, what questions would you ask him? Discuss with a partner.

12D Dare to disagree

TEDTALKS

MARGARET HEFFERNAN is an entrepreneur, a writer, and the former CEO of several companies. She studies how organizations think—in particular, how an all-too-common culture of conflict avoidance can lead organizations and managers astray.

Margaret Heffernan's idea worth spreading is that if we want the best results at work, we can't be afraid to challenge our colleagues and must dare to disagree with conventional wisdom.

PREVIEWING

Read the paragraph below. Match each **bold** word to its meaning. You will hear these words in the TED Talk.

Alice Stewart was a British physician and a pioneer in social medicine. After World War II, she specialized in the study of childhood leukemia. She found that the practice of X-raying pregnant women was causing leukemia in children. The medical community, afraid of the controversy this would **provoke**, strongly opposed her finding and tried to **disprove** it. Stewart became **embroiled** in a 25-year battle to get her research recognized. Finally, in the 1970s, experts were persuaded and the practice of X-raying pregnant women was stopped.

1 to show to be incorrect   _____

2 deeply involved in a difficult situation   _____

3 to cause a reaction, especially a negative one   _____

VIEWING

A ▶ **12.9** Watch Part 1 of the TED Talk. Choose the correct options.

1 What made Alice Stewart and George Kneale good collaborators?

  a Both of them loved working with numbers.

  b Both of them were very friendly people.

  c Both of them were good at dealing with conflict.

2 Which of the following best summarizes their model of thinking?

  a Hard facts and statistics are more reliable than personal opinions.

  b Finding evidence that disproves a theory is just as important as finding evidence that confirms it.

  c Finding a middle ground compromise is crucial to resolving personality differences between co-workers.

B ▶ **12.10** Watch Part 2 of the TED Talk. Would Margaret Heffernan agree with the following statements? Circle **Y** for yes or **N** for no.

1 People who have similar points of view make the most effective collaborators.   **Y**   **N**

2 Constructive conflict requires a lot of patience and energy.   **Y**   **N**

3 The biggest problems we face have come from individuals, not organizations.   **Y**   **N**

4 A successful organization is one that knows how to avoid conflict.   **Y**   **N**

5 Many European and American executives are afraid to raise concerns at work.   **Y**   **N**

6 Many CEOs pay more attention to recruiting employees instead of examining the organization's culture and how it thinks.   **Y**   **N**

C ▶ **12.11** Watch Part 3 of the TED Talk. Match the terms used by Margaret Heffernan to their corresponding situations.

1 allies ○   ○ Pablo informed the media about a faulty product being manufactured by his company.

2 whistleblower ○   ○ Melissa is good at organizing and guiding teams as well as managing conflict.

3 crank ○   ○ A few of Pablo's colleagues share the same concerns as him and are on his side.

4 leader ○   ○ Gina is a very negative and bad-tempered person, and seems to like to cause conflict.

D CRITICAL THINKING

Inferring **Discuss these questions with a partner. Then compare answers with your classmates.**

1 Margaret Heffernan says, "It's a fantastic model of collaboration—thinking partners who aren't echo chambers." What does she mean by this?

2 What is Heffernan's opinion of whistleblowers?

VOCABULARY IN CONTEXT

A ▶ **12.12** Watch the excerpts from the TED Talk. Choose the correct meaning of the words.

B Complete the sentences with the words from the box.

crunch data	dare to	bound to	stand up to

1 Surveys show that employees these days are increasingly willing to report corruption and wrongdoing. Whistleblowing is therefore _____ increase.

2 Thanks to new computer software, we can _____ faster than ever before.

3 Increased legal protection will give workers more confidence to _____ their employers.

4 If you were a whistleblower, would you _____ reveal your identity?

PRESENTATION SKILLS Using pauses

Using pauses in your presentation is an effective way to emphasize your main points.

- Pause when you want to draw the audience's attention to your next point. Maintain eye contact with your audience to show that the pause is intentional.
- Pause at the end of a point to give the audience time to process what you have said.
- Pause after a joke to allow the audience time to laugh.
- Pause when you show a new slide to give the audience time to read it.

A ▶ **12.13** Watch part of Margaret Heffernan's TED Talk. Mark with a **/** where she pauses in each excerpt below.

1 "Because it was only by not being able to prove that she was wrong, that George could give Alice the confidence she needed to know that she was right."

2 "It's a fantastic model of collaboration—thinking partners who aren't echo chambers. I wonder how many of us have, or dare to have, such collaborators."

3 "So how do organizations think? Well, for the most part, they don't. And that isn't because they don't want to, it's really because they can't. And they can't because the people inside of them are too afraid of conflict."

4 "In surveys of European and American executives, fully 85 percent of them acknowledged that they had issues or concerns at work that they were afraid to raise."

B Work in pairs. Look at the paragraph about Alice Stewart on page 159. Imagine this is part of a presentation you are giving. Mark with a **/** where you think you should pause. Then compare and discuss your answers with your partner.

C Work with a new partner. Think of a time when you disagreed with someone. It could be a friend, a family member, or a teacher. Make notes about the story. Then tell the story to your partner, using pauses where effective.

❝ I think we need to be teaching these skills to kids and adults at every stage of their development. ❞

12E What should we do?

COMMUNICATE A company meeting

A Work in pairs. You and your partner work for a company that produces food products. An employee has discovered that a chemical is being added to the products to make them tastier. The chemical has been banned in several countries but not yours. There is mixed evidence about its health risks to consumers. **Student A:** You are the senior manager. Turn to page 167. **Student B:** You are the employee. Turn to page 168.

B Student A is meeting Student B to discuss what to do next. Follow the steps below. You may take notes if necessary.

> **1** Student A: Welcome Student B to the meeting.
>
> **2** Student B: Explain your concerns to Student A and what you think the company should do.
>
> **3** Student A: As you listen to Student B, apply the RASA techniques (page 136). Then suggest ways to solve the problem.
>
> **4** Student B: As you listen to Student A, apply the RASA techniques (page 136).
>
> **5** Try to reach an agreement on what to do to fix the problem.

Suggesting solutions to a problem

Let's find out more about ...   *Maybe we should ...*

I think we should stop using the chemical immediately and recall all the products.

Yes, I have temporarily halted production and ordered everyone to stop using the chemical. But before we recall the product, let's find out more about the health risks.

C Share the results of your discussion with your classmates. What are the different solutions suggested?

WRITING An email

Write an email to the CEO of the company, explaining your role and the decisions reached. Give your reasons.

Dear Mr. Jones,

I met with _____ today to discuss the problem as you requested, and we were able to come to an agreement. We have decided that we need to ...

An internal company meeting

Presentation 4

MODEL PRESENTATION

A Complete the transcript of the presentation using the words in the box.

rushing	get away	suggested that	hadn't gone
a few	high-stress	relationships	leisurely

Hi, everybody. I'm Brenda. Tell me, how many of you sometimes feel like there aren't enough hours in the day? Right, almost everyone. I know exactly how you feel. I'm a newspaper reporter. It's a ¹_____ job that keeps me very busy, so I often feel like I'm ²_____ through life instead of actually living it.

³_____ months ago, I decided I needed to ⁴_____ from work for a while and take a vacation. A friend ⁵_____ I go to El Nido in the Philippines. Some of you may not have heard of it before. El Nido is a coastal town that's known for its white-sand beaches and clear waters. My sister came with me, and we stayed in a beautiful resort. We took long,

⁶_____ walks together, and went snorkeling and scuba diving. Picture yourself on a beach, feeling the warm sun on your face. After spending a couple of days like that, I felt refreshed and so much happier.

If I ⁷_____ on this trip, I'm sure I'd be even more stressed out now and less productive at work. So my advice to all of you is to slow down, develop more meaningful ⁸_____ with your loved ones, and spend more time interacting with nature. Thanks for listening.

B ▶ **P.4** Watch the presentation and check your answers.

C ▶ **P.4** Review the list of presentation skills from Units 1–12 below. Which does the speaker use? Check (✓) them as you watch again. Then compare with a partner.

The speaker …
- [ ] asks the audience questions
- [ ] asks the audience to imagine themselves in a particular situation
- [ ] uses examples the audience is familiar with
- [ ] uses props
- [ ] begins with a strong statement
- [ ] explains technical words that the audience may not understand
- [ ] raises their hand above their head
- [ ] includes a quote
- [ ] smiles and shows enthusiasm while presenting
- [ ] pauses after asking a question to give the audience time to reflect

YOUR TURN

A You are going to plan and give a short presentation about a vacation spot that encourages people to slow down and enjoy nature. Think of the location, what activities you can do there, and how visiting this place will benefit people. Make notes in the chart below.

Location	
Activities	
Benefits	

B Look at the useful phrases in the box below. Think about which ones you will need in your presentation.

> **Useful phrases**
>
> **Asking the audience questions:** *Tell me, how many of you ...?*
> *Would you like to ...?*
>
> **Describing places:** *beautiful, picturesque, unspoiled, peaceful*
>
> **Explaining the benefits of something:** *This will help ...*
> *... is a good idea for people who ...*

C Work with a partner. Take turns giving your presentation using your notes. Use some of the presentation skills from Units 1–12 below. As you listen, check (✓) each skill your partner uses.

> The speaker ...
> ☐ asks the audience questions
> ☐ asks the audience to imagine themselves in a particular situation
> ☐ uses examples the audience is familiar with
> ☐ uses props
> ☐ begins with a strong statement
> ☐ explains technical words that the audience may not understand
> ☐ raises their hand above their head
> ☐ includes a quote
> ☐ smiles and shows enthusiasm while presenting
> ☐ pauses after asking a question to give the audience time to reflect

D Give your partner some feedback on their talk. Include at least two things you liked and one thing that could be improved.

Communication Activities

1B   SPEAKING

Find a person for each of the descriptions in the chart. Write their names and ask a follow-up question to get more information. Use the verbs in the box to help you.

| likes | prefers | enjoys | wants |

Find someone who deals with stress by ...	Name	More information
eating.		
hanging out with friends.		
sleeping.		
exercising.		
watching movies and TV.		
listening to music.		
going online (checking social media, etc.).		
playing with a pet (cat, dog).		
cooking.		
playing video games.		

Do you like exercising when you're stressed?

Yes, I do.

Do you prefer to exercise in a gym or outdoors?

3E   COMMUNICATE

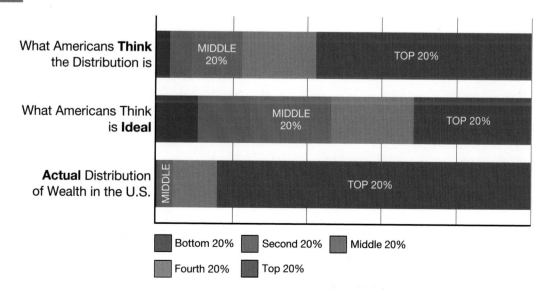

What Americans **Think** the Distribution is

What Americans Think is **Ideal**

Actual Distribution of Wealth in the U.S.

Bottom 20%   Second 20%   Middle 20%   Fourth 20%   Top 20%

Decide which photograph below is real and which is fake. Discuss your answers with a partner.

A

B

A Complete the chart. Make some notes about things you did yesterday—both big and small. This should include when you woke up, meals you ate, places you went to, and activities you did.

Time	Activity	Time	Activity
6 a.m.		4 p.m.	
8 a.m.		6 p.m.	
10 a.m.		8 p.m.	
12 p.m.		10 p.m.	
2 p.m.		12 a.m.	

B Work in groups of three or four. Talk about what you had done by certain times yesterday.

> By 8 a.m., I'd eaten breakfast and gone to the gym.

> By 12 p.m., I'd studied for three hours and written a report.

C In your group, discuss the questions below.

1 Who had the most interesting day?

2 Who had the busiest day?

12E COMMUNICATE

STUDENT A

You are the senior manager. You weren't aware that a potentially dangerous chemical has been added to the food products. You have been instructed by the CEO to resolve this issue without damaging the company's reputation if possible, so you need to persuade the employee not to talk to the media. Think about what you can do to solve the problem. Consider the ideas below or think of your own.

- Stop using the chemical immediately.
- Launch an internal investigation to find out who had knowledge of the chemical use.
- Conduct tests to find out more about the chemical's health risks to consumers.
- Promote the employee to a new position in the company.

STUDENT B

You are the employee. You have found out that a potentially dangerous chemical has been added to the food products, but you haven't told anyone else apart from your manager. You don't want to lose your job, but you also feel that the company should take responsibility for what has happened and acknowledge the problem. Think about what you want your manager to do. Consider the ideas below or think of your own.

- Recall all the food products in the market immediately.
- Issue a press release to apologize to the public and describe how the problem is being addressed.
- Launch an investigation to find out who had knowledge of the chemical use.
- Establish formal procedures to protect whistleblowers.

Unit 1 Kelly McGonigal: How to make stress your friend

Part 1

For years I've been telling people, stress makes you sick. It increases the risk of everything from the common cold to cardiovascular disease. Basically, I've turned stress into the enemy. But I have changed my mind about stress, and today, I want to change yours.

Let me start with the study that made me rethink my whole approach to stress. This study tracked 30,000 adults in the United States for eight years, and they started by asking people, "How much stress have you experienced in the last year?" They also asked, "Do you believe that stress is harmful for your health?" And then they used public death records to find out who died.

(Laughter)

OK. Some bad news first. People who experienced a lot of stress in the previous year had a 43 percent increased risk of dying. But that was only true for the people who also believed that stress is harmful for your health.

(Laughter)

People who experienced a lot of stress but did not view stress as harmful were no more likely to die. In fact, they had the lowest risk of dying of anyone in the study, including people who had relatively little stress.

[…] So this study got me wondering: Can changing how you think about stress make you healthier? And here the science says yes. When you change your mind about stress, you can change your body's response to stress.

Part 2

Now to explain how this works, I want you all to pretend that you are participants in a study designed to stress you out. It's called the social stress test. You come into the laboratory, and you're told you have to give a five-minute impromptu speech on your personal weaknesses to a panel of expert evaluators sitting right in front of you, and to make sure you feel the pressure, there are bright lights and a camera in your face, kind of like this.

(Laughter)

And the evaluators have been trained to give you discouraging, non-verbal feedback, like this.

(Exhales)

(Laughter)

[…] If you were actually in this study, you'd probably be a little stressed out. Your heart might be pounding, you might be breathing faster, maybe breaking out into a sweat. And normally, we interpret these physical changes as anxiety or signs that we aren't coping very well with the pressure.

But what if you viewed them instead as signs that your body was energized, was preparing you to meet this challenge? Now that is exactly what participants were told in a study conducted at Harvard University.

[…] Now, in a typical stress response, your heart rate goes up, and your blood vessels constrict like this. And this is one of the reasons that chronic stress is sometimes associated with cardiovascular disease. It's not really healthy to be in this state all the time. But in the study, when participants viewed their stress response as helpful, their blood vessels stayed relaxed like this. Their heart was still pounding, but this is a much healthier cardiovascular profile. It actually looks a lot like what happens in moments of joy and courage. Over a lifetime of stressful experiences, this one biological change could be the difference between a stress-induced heart attack at age 50 and living well into your 90s. And this is really what the new science of stress reveals, that how you think about stress matters.

So my goal as a health psychologist has changed. I no longer want to get rid of your stress. I want to make you better at stress.

Part 3

I want to finish by telling you about one more study. And listen up, because this study could also save a life. This study tracked about 1,000 adults in the United States, and they ranged in age from 34 to 93, and they started the study by asking, "How much stress have you experienced in the last year?" They also asked, "How much time have you spent helping out friends, neighbors, people in your community?" And then they used public records for the next five years to find out who died.

OK, so the bad news first: For every major stressful life experience, like financial difficulties or family crisis, that increased the risk of dying by 30 percent. But— and I hope you are expecting a "but" by now—but that wasn't true for everyone. People who spent time caring for others showed absolutely no stress-related increase in dying. Zero. Caring created resilience.

And so we see once again that the harmful effects of stress on your health are not inevitable. How you think and how you act can transform your experience of stress. When you choose to view your stress response as helpful, you create the biology of courage. And when you choose to connect with others under stress, you can create resilience. Now I wouldn't necessarily ask for more stressful experiences in my life, but this science has given me a whole new appreciation for stress.

[…] Thank you.

Unit 2 Colin Stokes: How movies teach manhood

Part 1

You know, my favorite part of being a dad is the movies I get to watch. I love sharing my favorite movies with my kids, and when my daughter was four, we got to watch *The Wizard of Oz* together. It totally dominated her imagination for months. Her favorite character was Glinda, of course. It gave her a great excuse to wear a sparkly dress and carry a wand.

But you watch that movie enough times, and you start to realize how unusual it is. Now we live today, and are raising our children, in a kind of children's-fantasy-spectacular-industrial complex. But *The Wizard of Oz* stood alone. It did not start that trend. Forty years later was when the trend really caught on, with, interestingly, another movie that featured a metal guy and a furry guy rescuing a girl by dressing up as the enemy's guards. Do you know what I'm talking about? (Laughter) Yeah.

Now, there's a big difference between these two movies, a couple of really big differences between *The Wizard of Oz* and all the movies we watch today. One is there's very little violence in *The Wizard of Oz*. The monkeys are rather aggressive, as are the apple trees. But I think if *The Wizard of Oz* were made today, the wizard would say, "Dorothy, you are the savior of Oz that the prophecy foretold. Use your magic slippers to defeat the computer-generated armies of the Wicked Witch." But that's not how it happens.

Another thing that's really unique about *The Wizard of Oz* to me is that all of the most heroic and wise and even villainous characters are female.

Part 2

Now I started to notice this when I actually showed *Star Wars* to my daughter, which was years later, and the situation was different. At that point, I also had a son. He was only three at the time. He was not invited to the screening. He was too young for that. But he was the second child, and the level of supervision had plummeted. (Laughter) So he wandered in, and it imprinted on him like a mommy duck does to its duckling, and I don't think he understands what's going on, but he is sure soaking in it.

And I wonder what he's soaking in. Is he picking up on the themes of courage and perseverance and loyalty? Is he picking up on the fact that Luke joins an army to overthrow the government? Is he picking up on the fact that there are only boys in the universe except for Aunt Beru, and of course this princess, who's really cool, but who kind of waits around through most of the movie so that she can award the hero with a medal and a wink to thank him for saving the universe, which he does by the magic that he was born with?

Compare this to 1939 with *The Wizard of Oz*. How does Dorothy win her movie? By making friends with everybody and being a leader. That's kind of the world I'd rather raise my kids in—Oz, right?—and not the world of dudes fighting, which is where we kind of have to be. Why is there so much Force—capital F, Force—in the movies we have for our kids, and so little yellow brick road?

[…] The movies are very, very focused on defeating the villain and getting your reward, and there's not a lot of room for other relationships and other journeys. It's almost as though if you're a boy, you are a dopey animal, and if you are a girl, you should bring your warrior costume. There are plenty of exceptions, and I will defend the Disney princesses in front of any of you. But they do send a message to boys, that they are not, the boys are not really the target audience. They are doing a phenomenal job of teaching girls how to defend against the patriarchy, but they are not necessarily showing boys how they're supposed to defend against the patriarchy. There's no models for them. And we also have some terrific women who are writing new stories for our kids, and as three-dimensional and delightful as Hermione and Katniss are, these are still war movies.

Part 3

Now, almost none of these movies pass the Bechdel Test. I don't know if you've heard of this. It has not yet caught on and caught fire, but maybe today we will start a movement. Alison Bechdel is a comic book artist, and back in the mid-'80s, she recorded this conversation she'd had with a friend about assessing the movies that they saw. And it's very simple. There's just three questions you should ask:

Is there more than one character in the movie that is female who has lines? So try to meet that bar.

And do these women talk to each other at any point in the movie?

And is their conversation about something other than the guy that they both like? (Laughter)

Right? Thank you. (Applause) Thank you very much.

Two women who exist and talk to each other about stuff. It does happen. I've seen it, and yet I very rarely see it in the movies that we know and love.

[...] I think our job in the Netflix queue is to look out for those movies that pass the Bechdel Test, if we can find them, and to seek out the heroines who are there, who show real courage, who bring people together, and to nudge our sons to identify with those heroines and to say, "I want to be on their team," because they're going to be on their team.

[...] I want more quests like that. I want fewer quests where my son is told, "Go out and fight it alone," and more quests where he sees that it's his job to join a team, maybe a team led by women, to help other people become better and be better people, like the Wizard of Oz. Thank you.

Unit 3 Hans Rosling: Global population growth, box by box

Part 1

I still remember the day in school when our teacher told us that the world population had become three billion people, and that was in 1960. I'm going to talk now about how world population has changed from that year and into the future, but I will not use digital technology, as I've done during my first five TED Talks. Instead, I have progressed, and I am, today, launching a brand new analog teaching technology that I picked up from IKEA: this box.

This box contains one billion people. And our teacher told us that the industrialized world, 1960, had one billion people. In the developing world, she said, they had two billion people. And they lived away then. There was a big gap between the one billion in the industrialized world and the two billion in the developing world. In the industrialized world, people were healthy, educated, rich, and they had small families. And their aspiration was to buy a car. And in 1960, all Swedes were saving to try to buy a Volvo like this. This was the economic level at which Sweden was. But in contrast to this, in the developing world, far away, the aspiration of the average family there was to have food for the day. They were saving to be able to buy a pair of shoes. There was an enormous gap in the world when I grew up. And this gap between the West and the rest has created a mindset of the world, which we still use linguistically when we talk about "the West" and "the Developing World." But the world has changed, and it's overdue to upgrade that mindset and that taxonomy of the world, and to understand it.

Part 2

But the world has changed, and it's overdue to upgrade that mindset and that taxonomy of the world, and to understand it.

And that's what I'm going to show you, because since 1960 what has happened in the world up to 2010 is that a staggering four billion people have been added to the world population. Just look how many. The world population has doubled since I went to school. And of course, there's been economic growth in the West. A lot of companies have happened to grow the economy, so the Western population moved over to here. And now their aspiration is not only to have a car. Now they want to have a holiday on a very remote destination and they want to fly. So this is where they are today. And the most successful of the developing countries, they have moved on, you know, and they have become emerging economies, we call them. They are now buying cars. And what happened a month ago was that the Chinese company, Geely, they acquired the Volvo company, and then finally the Swedes understood that something big had happened in the world. (Laughter)

So there they are. And the tragedy is that the two billion over here that is struggling for food and shoes, they are still almost as poor as they were 50 years ago. The new thing is that we have the biggest pile of billions, the three billions here, which are also becoming emerging economies, because they are quite healthy, relatively well-educated, and they already also have two to three children per woman, as those [richer also] have. And their aspiration now is, of course, to buy a bicycle, and then later on they would like to have a motorbike also. But this is the world we have today, no longer any gap. But the distance from the poorest here, the very poorest, to the very richest over here is wider than ever. But there is a continuous world from walking, biking, driving, flying—there are people on all levels, and most people tend to be somewhere in the middle. This is the new world we have today in 2010.

Part 3

Here I have on the screen my country bubbles. Every bubble is a country. The size is population. The colors show the continent. The yellow on there is the Americas; dark blue is Africa; brown is Europe; green is the Middle East; and this light blue is South Asia. That's India and this is China. Size is population. Here I have children per woman: two children, four children, six children, eight children—big families, small families. The year is 1960. And down here, child survival, the percentage of children surviving childhood up to starting school: 60 percent, 70 percent, 80 percent, 90, and almost 100 percent, as we have today in the wealthiest and healthiest countries. But look, this is the world my teacher talked about in 1960: one billion Western world here—high child-survival, small families—and all the rest, the rainbow of developing countries, with very large families and poor child survival.

What has happened? I start the world. Here we go. Can you see, as the years pass by, child survival is increasing? They get soap, hygiene, education, vaccination, penicillin, and then family planning. Family size is decreasing. [When] they get up to 90-percent child survival, then families decrease, and most of the Arab countries in the Middle East is falling down there [to small families]. Look, Bangladesh catching up with India. The whole emerging world joins the Western world with good child survival and small family size, but we still have the poorest billion. Can you see the poorest billion, those [two] boxes I had over here? They are still up here. And they still have a child survival of only 70 to 80 percent, meaning that if you have six children born, there will be at least four who survive to the next generation. And the population will double in one generation.

So the only way of really getting world population [growth] to stop is to continue to improve child survival to 90 percent. That's why investments by Gates Foundation, UNICEF, and aid organizations, together with national government in the poorest countries, are so good; because they are actually helping us to reach a sustainable population size of the world. We can stop at nine billion if we do the right things. Child survival is the new green. It's only by child survival that we will stop population growth. And will it happen? Well, I'm not an optimist, neither am I a pessimist. I'm a very serious "possibilist." It's a new category where we take emotion apart, and we just work analytically with the world. It can be done. We can have a much more just world. With green technology and with investments to alleviate poverty, and global governance, the world can become like this.

And look at the position of the old West. Remember when this blue box was all alone, leading the world, living its own life. This will not happen [again]. The role of the old West in the new world is to become the foundation of the modern world—nothing more, nothing less. But it's a very important role. Do it well and get used to it.

Thank you very much.

Unit 4 Pamela Meyer: How to spot a liar

Part 1

OK, now I don't want to alarm anybody in this room, but it's just come to my attention that the person to your right is a liar.

(Laughter)

Also, the person to your left is a liar. Also, the person sitting in your very seats is a liar. We're all liars. What I'm going to do today is I'm going to show you what the research says about why we're all liars, how you can become a liespotter, and why you might want to go the extra mile and go from liespotting to truth seeking, and ultimately to trust building.

[…] And we all kind of hate to admit it. We wish we were better husbands, better wives, smarter, more powerful, taller, richer—the list goes on. Lying is an attempt to bridge that gap, to connect our wishes and our fantasies about who we wish we were, how we wish we could be, with what we're really like. And boy are we willing to fill in those gaps in our lives with lies.

On a given day, studies show that you may be lied to anywhere from 10 to 200 times. Now granted, many of those are white lies. But in another study, it showed that strangers lied three times within the first 10 minutes of meeting each other.

(Laughter)

Now when we first hear this data, we recoil. We can't believe how prevalent lying is. We're essentially against lying. But if you look more closely, the plot actually thickens. We lie more to strangers than we lie to co-workers. Extroverts lie more than introverts. Men lie eight times more about themselves than they do other people. Women lie more to protect other people. If you're an average married couple, you're going to lie to your spouse in one out of every 10 interactions. Now, you may think that's bad. If you're unmarried, that number drops to three.

Part 2

Trained liespotters get to the truth 90 percent of the time. The rest of us, we're only 54 percent accurate. Why is it so easy to learn? Well, there are good liars and there are bad liars. There are no real original liars. We all make the same mistakes. We all use the same techniques.

[…] Now this brings us to our next pattern, which is body language. With body language, here's what you've got to do. You've really got to just throw your assumptions out the door. Let the science temper your knowledge a little bit. Because we think liars fidget all the time. Well guess what, they're known to freeze their upper bodies when they're lying. We think liars won't look you in the eyes. Well guess what, they look you in the eyes a little too much just to compensate for that myth. We think warmth and smiles convey honesty, sincerity. But a trained liespotter can spot a fake smile a mile away. Can you all spot the fake smile here? You can consciously contract the muscles in your cheeks. But the real smile's in the eyes, the crow's feet of the eyes. They cannot be consciously contracted, especially if you overdid the Botox. Don't overdo the Botox; nobody will think you're honest.

Now we're going to look at the hot spots. Can you tell what's happening in a conversation? Can you start to find the hot spots to see the discrepancies between someone's words and someone's actions? Now, I know it seems really obvious, but when you're having a conversation with someone that you suspect of deception, attitude is by far the most overlooked but telling of indicators.

Part 3

An honest person is going to be cooperative. They're going to show they're on your side. They're going to be enthusiastic. They're going to be willing and helpful to getting you to the truth. They're going to be willing to brainstorm, name suspects, provide details. They're going to say, "Hey, maybe it was those guys in payroll that forged those checks." They're going to be infuriated if they sense they're wrongly accused throughout the entire course of the interview, not just in flashes; they'll be infuriated throughout the entire course of the interview. And if you ask someone honest what should happen to whomever did forge those checks, an honest person is much more likely to recommend strict rather than lenient punishment.

Now let's say you're having that exact same conversation with someone deceptive. That person may be withdrawn, look down, lower their voice, pause, be kind of herky-jerky. Ask a deceptive person to tell their story, they're going to pepper it with way too much detail in all kinds of irrelevant places. And then they're going to tell their story in strict chronological order. And what a trained interrogator does is they come in and in very subtle ways over the course of several hours, they will ask that person to tell their story backwards, and then they'll watch them squirm, and track which questions produce the highest volume of deceptive tells.

Why do they do that? Well, we all do the same thing. We rehearse our words, but we rarely rehearse our gestures. We say "yes," we shake our heads "no." We tell very convincing stories, we slightly shrug our shoulders. We commit terrible crimes, and we smile at the delight in getting away with it.

[…] Science has surfaced many, many more indicators. We know, for example, we know liars will shift their blink rate, point their feet towards an exit.

[…] They'll alter their vocal tone, often making their vocal tone much lower.

Now here's the deal. These behaviors are just behaviors. They're not proof of deception. They're red flags.

[…] When you combine the science of recognizing deception with the art of looking, listening, you exempt yourself from collaborating in a lie. You start up that path of being just a little bit more explicit, because you signal to everyone around you, you say, "Hey, my world, our world, it's going to be an honest one. My world is going to be one where truth is strengthened and falsehood is recognized and marginalized." And when you do that, the ground around you starts to shift just a little bit.

And that's the truth. Thank you.

(Applause)

Unit 5 David Blaine: How I held my breath for 17 minutes

Part 1

As a young magician, I was obsessed with Houdini and his underwater challenges. So, I began, early on, competing against the other kids, seeing how long I could stay underwater while they went up and down to breathe, you know, five times, while I stayed under on one breath. By the time I was a teenager, I was able to hold my breath for three minutes and 30 seconds. I would later find out that was Houdini's personal record.

[…] So, I started researching into pearl divers. You know, because they go down for four minutes on one breath. And when I was researching pearl divers, I found the world of free-diving. It was the most amazing thing that I ever discovered, pretty much. There is many different aspects to free-diving. There is depth records, where people go as deep as they can. And then there is static apnea. That's holding your breath as long as you can in one place without moving. That was the one that I studied.

The first thing that I learned is when you're holding your breath, you should never move at all; that wastes energy. And that depletes oxygen, and it builds up CO_2 in your blood. So, I learned never to move. And I learned how to slow my heart rate down. I had to remain perfectly still and just relax and think that I wasn't in my body, and just control that. And then I learned how to purge. Purging is basically hyperventilating. You blow in and out—

(Breathing loudly)

You do that, you get lightheaded, you get tingling. And you're really ridding your body of CO_2. So, when you hold your breath, it's infinitely easier. Then I learned that you have to take a huge breath, and just hold and relax and never let any air out, and just hold and relax through all the pain.

Part 2

I started learning about the world record holder. His name is Tom Sietas. And this guy is perfectly built for holding his breath. He's six foot four. He's 160 pounds. And his total lung capacity is twice the size of an average person. I'm six foot one, and fat. We'll say big-boned.

(Laughter)

I had to drop 50 pounds in three months. So, everything that I put into my body, I considered as medicine. Every bit of food was exactly what it was for its nutritional value. I ate really small, controlled portions throughout the day. And I started to really adapt my body.

[Individual results may vary.]

(Laughter)

The thinner I was, the longer I was able to hold my breath. And by eating so well and training so hard, my resting heart rate dropped to 38 beats per minute. Which is lower than most Olympic athletes. In four months of training, I was able to hold my breath for over seven minutes. I wanted to try holding my breath everywhere. I wanted to try it in the most extreme situations to see if I could slow my heart rate down under duress.

(Laughter)

I decided that I was going to break the world record live on primetime television.

[...] So, I started full focus. I completely trained to get my breath-hold time up for what I needed to do. But there was no way to prepare for the live television aspect of it, being on Oprah. But in practice, I would do it facedown, floating on the pool. But for TV they wanted me to be upright so they could see my face, basically. The other problem was the suit was so buoyant that they had to strap my feet in to keep me from floating up. So, I had to use my legs to hold my feet into the straps that were loose, which was a real problem for me. That made me extremely nervous, raising the heart rate.

Part 3

When I made it to the halfway mark, at eight minutes, I was 100 percent certain that I was not going to be able to make this. There was no way for me to do it.

[...] I kept pushing to 10 minutes. At 10 minutes you start getting all these really strong tingling sensations in your fingers and toes. And I knew that that was blood shunting, when the blood rushes away from your extremities to provide oxygen to your vital organs. At 11 minutes I started feeling throbbing sensations in my legs, and my lips started to feel really strange.

[...] At 15 minutes I was suffering major O_2 deprivation to the heart. And I started having ischemia to the heart. My heartbeat would go from 120 to 50, to 150, to 40, to 20, to 150 again. It would skip a beat. It would start. It would stop. And I felt all this. And I was sure that I was going to have a heart attack.

So, at 16 minutes what I did is I slid my feet out because I knew that if I did go out, if I did have a heart attack, they'd have to jump into the binding and take my feet out before pulling me up. I was really nervous. I let my feet out, and I started floating to the top. And I didn't take my head out. But I was just floating there waiting for my heart to stop, just waiting. They had doctors with the "Pst," you know, sitting there waiting. And then suddenly I hear screaming. And I think that there is some weird thing—that I had died or something had happened. And then I realized that I had made it to 16:32. So, with the energy of

everybody that was there, I decided to keep pushing. And I went to 17 minutes and four seconds.

(Applause)

[...] As a magician, I try to show things to people that seem impossible. And I think magic, whether I'm holding my breath or shuffling a deck of cards, is pretty simple. It's practice, it's training, and it's—It's practice, it's training and experimenting, while pushing through the pain to be the best that I can be. And that's what magic is to me, so, thank you.

Unit 6 Bill and Melinda Gates: Why giving away our wealth has been the most satisfying thing we've done

Part 1

Chris Anderson: Bringing up three children when you're the world's richest family seems like a social experiment without much prior art. How have you managed it? What's been your approach?

Bill Gates: Well, I'd say overall the kids get a great education, but you've got to make sure they have a sense of their own ability and what they're going to go and do, and our philosophy has been to be very clear with them—most of the money's going to the foundation—and help them find something they're excited about. We want to strike a balance where they have the freedom to do anything but not a lot of money showered on them so they could go out and do nothing. And so far, they're fairly diligent, excited to pick their own direction.

CA: You've obviously guarded their privacy carefully for obvious reasons. I'm curious why you've given me permission to show this picture now here at TED.

Melinda Gates: Well, it's interesting. As they get older, they so know that our family belief is about responsibility, that we are in an unbelievable situation just to live in the United States and have a great education, and we have a responsibility to give back to the world. And so as they get older and we are teaching them—they have been to so many countries around the world—they're saying, you know, we do want people to know that we believe in what you're doing, Mom and Dad, and it is okay to show us more. So we have their permission to show this picture, and I think Paul Farmer is probably going to put it eventually in some of his work. But they really care deeply about the mission of the foundation, too.

CA: You've easily got enough money despite your vast contributions to the foundation to make them all billionaires. Is that your plan for them?

BG: Nope. No. They won't have anything like that. They need to have a sense that their own work is meaningful and important. We read an article long, actually, before we got married, where Warren Buffett talked about that, and we're quite convinced that it wasn't a favor either to society or to the kids.

Part 2

CA: And I think you've pledged that by the time you're done, more than, or 95 percent of your wealth, will be given to the foundation.

BG: Yes.

CA: And since this relationship, it's amazing— (Applause) And recently, you and Warren have been going around trying to persuade other billionaires and successful people to pledge to give, what, more than half of their assets for philanthropy. How is that going?

BG: Well, we've got about 120 people who have now taken this giving pledge. The thing that's great is that we get together yearly and talk about, OK, do you hire staff, what do you give to them? We're not trying to homogenize it. I mean, the beauty of philanthropy is this mind-blowing diversity. People give to some things. We look and go, "Wow." But that's great. That's the role of philanthropy is to pick different approaches, including even in one space, like education. We need more experimentation. But it's been wonderful, meeting those people, sharing their journey to philanthropy, how they involve their kids, where they're doing it differently, and it's been way more successful than we expected. Now it looks like it'll just keep growing in size in the years ahead.

MG: And having people see that other people are making change with philanthropy, I mean, these are people who have created their own businesses, put their own ingenuity behind incredible ideas. If they put their ideas and their brain behind philanthropy, they can change the world. And they start to see others doing it, and saying, "Wow, I want to do that with my own money." To me, that's the piece that's incredible.

Part 3

CA: It seems to me, it's actually really hard for some people to figure out even how to remotely spend that much money on something else. There are probably some billionaires in the room and certainly some successful people. I'm curious, can you make the pitch? What's the pitch?

BG: Well, it's the most fulfilling thing we've ever done, and you can't take it with you, and if it's not good for your kids, then let's get together and brainstorm about what can be done. The world is a far better place because of the philanthropists of the past, and the U.S. tradition here, which is the strongest, is the envy of the world. And part of the reason I'm so optimistic is because I do think philanthropy is going to grow and take some of these things government's just not good at working on and discovering and shine some light in the right direction.

CA: The world's got this terrible inequality, growing inequality problem that seems structural. It does seem to me that if more of your peers took the approach that you two have made, it would make a dent both in that problem and certainly in the perception of that problem. Is that a fair comment?

BG: Oh yeah. If you take from the most wealthy and give to the least wealthy, it's good. It tries to balance out, and that's just.

MG: But you change systems. In the U.S., we're trying to change the education system so it's just for everybody and it works for all students. That, to me, really changes the inequality balance.

BG: That's the most important. (Applause)

Unit 7 David Sengeh: The sore problem of prosthetic limbs

Part 1

I was born and raised in Sierra Leone, a small and very beautiful country in West Africa, a country rich both in physical resources and creative talent.

However, Sierra Leone is infamous for a decade-long rebel war in the '90s when entire villages were burnt down. An estimated 8,000 men, women, and children had their arms and legs amputated during this time. As my family and I ran for safety when I was about 12 from one of those attacks, I resolved that I would do everything I could to ensure that my own children would not go through the same experiences we had. They would, in fact, be part of a Sierra Leone where war and amputation were no longer a strategy for gaining power.

As I watched people who I knew, loved ones, recover from this devastation, one thing that deeply troubled me was that many of the amputees in the country would not use their prostheses. The reason, I would come to find out, was that their prosthetic sockets were painful because they did not fit well.

Part 2

The prosthetic socket is the part in which the amputee inserts their residual limb, and which connects to the prosthetic ankle. Even in the developed world, it takes a period of three weeks to often years for a patient to get a comfortable socket, if ever. Prosthetists still use conventional processes like molding and casting to create single-material prosthetic sockets. Such sockets often leave intolerable amounts of pressure on the limbs of the patient, leaving them with pressure sores and blisters. It does not matter how powerful your prosthetic ankle is. If your prosthetic socket is uncomfortable, you will not use your leg, and that is just simply unacceptable in our age.

So one day, when I met Professor Hugh Herr about two and a half years ago, and he asked me if I knew how to solve this problem, I said, "No, not yet, but I would love to figure it out." And so, for my Ph.D. at the MIT Media Lab, I designed custom prosthetic sockets quickly and cheaply that are more comfortable than conventional prostheses. I used magnetic resonance imaging to capture the actual shape of the patient's anatomy, then use finite element modeling to better predict the internal stresses and strains on the normal forces, and then create a prosthetic socket for manufacture. We use a 3-D printer to create a multi-material prosthetic socket which relieves pressure where needed on the anatomy of the patient. In short, we're using data to make novel sockets quickly and cheaply.

Part 3

Disability in our age should not prevent anyone from living meaningful lives. My hope and desire is that the tools and processes we develop in our research group can be used to bring highly functional prostheses to those who need them. For me, a place to begin healing the souls of those affected by war and disease is by creating comfortable and affordable interfaces for their bodies. Whether it's in Sierra Leone or in Boston, I hope this not only restores but indeed transforms their sense of human potential.

Thank you very much.

(Applause)

Unit 8 Meg Jay: Why 30 is not the new 20

Part 1

So, I specialize in 20-somethings because I believe that every single one of those 50 million 20-somethings deserves to know what psychologists, sociologists, neurologists, and fertility specialists already know: that claiming your 20s is one of the simplest, yet most transformative, things you can do for work, for love, for your happiness, maybe even for the world.

[…] I want to change what 20-somethings are doing and thinking.

Here's a story about how that can go. It's a story about a woman named Emma. At 25, Emma came to my office because she was, in her words, having an identity crisis. She said she thought she might like to work in art or entertainment, but she hadn't decided yet, so she'd spent the last few years waiting tables instead. Because it was cheaper, she lived with a boyfriend who displayed his temper more than his ambition. And as hard as her 20s were, her early life had been even harder. She often cried in our sessions, but then would collect herself by saying, "You can't pick your family, but you can pick your friends."

Well, one day, Emma comes in and she hangs her head in her lap, and she sobbed for most of the hour. She'd just bought a new address book, and she'd spent the morning filling in her many contacts, but then she'd been left staring at that empty blank that comes after the words "In case of emergency, please call …" She was nearly hysterical when she looked at me and said, "Who's going to be there for me if I get in a car wreck? Who's going to take care of me if I have cancer?"

Part 2

So over the next weeks and months, I told Emma three things that every 20-something, male or female, deserves to hear.

First, I told Emma to forget about having an identity crisis and get some identity capital. By "get identity capital," I mean do something that adds value to who you are. Do something that's an investment in who you might want to be next. I didn't know the future of Emma's career, and no one knows the future of work, but I do know this: Identity capital begets identity capital. So now is the time for that cross-country job, that internship, that startup you want to try. I'm not discounting 20-something exploration here, but I am discounting exploration that's not supposed to count, which, by the way, is not exploration. That's procrastination. I told Emma to explore work and make it count.

Second, I told Emma that the urban tribe is overrated. Best friends are great for giving rides to the airport, but 20-somethings who huddle together with like-minded peers limit who they know, what they know, how they think, how they speak, and where they work. That new piece of capital, that new person to date, almost always comes from outside the inner circle. New things come from what are called our weak ties, our friends of friends of friends. So yes, half of 20-somethings are un- or under-employed. But half aren't, and weak ties are how you get yourself into that group. Half of new jobs are never posted, so reaching out to your neighbor's boss is how you get that unposted job. It's not cheating. It's the science of how information spreads.

Last but not least, Emma believed that you can't pick your family, but you can pick your friends. Now this was true for her growing up, but as a 20-something, soon Emma would pick her family when she partnered with someone and created a family of her own. I told Emma the time to start picking your family is now.

Now you may be thinking that 30 is actually a better time to settle down than 20, or even 25, and I agree with you. But grabbing whoever you're living with or sleeping with when everyone on Facebook starts walking down the aisle is not progress. The best time to work on your marriage is before you have one, and that means being as intentional with love as you are with work. Picking your family is about consciously choosing who and what you want rather than just making it work or killing time with whoever happens to be choosing you.

Part 3

So what happened to Emma? Well, we went through that address book, and she found an old roommate's cousin who worked at an art museum in another state. That weak tie helped her get a job there. That job offer gave her the reason to leave that live-in boyfriend. Now, five years later, she's a special events planner for museums. She's married to a man she mindfully chose. She loves her new career, she loves her new family, and she sent me a card that said, "Now the emergency contact blanks don't seem big enough."

Now Emma's story made that sound easy, but that's what I love about working with 20-somethings. They are so easy to help. Twenty-somethings are like airplanes just leaving LAX, bound for somewhere west. Right after takeoff, a slight change in course is the difference between landing in Alaska or Fiji. Likewise, at 21 or 25 or even 29, one good conversation, one good break, one good TED Talk, can have an enormous effect across years and even generations to come.

So here's an idea worth spreading to every 20-something you know. It's as simple as what I learned to say to Alex. It's what I now have the privilege of saying to 20-somethings like Emma every single day: Thirty is not the new 20, so claim your adulthood, get some identity capital, use your weak ties, pick your family. Don't be defined by what you didn't know or didn't do. You're deciding your life right now.

Thank you.

(Applause)

Unit 9 Vijay Kumar: Robots that fly … and cooperate

Part 1

The robot I'm holding in my hand is this one, and it's been created by two students, Alex and Daniel. So this weighs a little more than a tenth of a pound. It consumes about 15 watts of power. And as you can see, it's about eight inches in diameter.

[…] So why build robots like this? Well, robots like this have many applications. You can send them inside buildings like this, as first responders to look for intruders, maybe look for biochemical leaks, gaseous leaks. You can also use them for applications like construction. So here are robots carrying beams, columns and assembling cube-like structures. I'll tell

you a little bit more about this. The robots can be used for transporting cargo. So one of the problems with these small robots is their payload-carrying capacity. So you might want to have multiple robots carry payloads. This is a picture of a recent experiment we did—actually not so recent anymore—in Sendai, shortly after the earthquake. So robots like this could be sent into collapsed buildings, to assess the damage after natural disasters, or sent into reactor buildings, to map radiation levels.

[…] Here, you have overhead motion-capture cameras on the top that tell the robot where it is 100 times a second. It also tells the robot where these obstacles are. And the obstacles can be moving. And here, you'll see Daniel throw this hoop into the air, while the robot is calculating the position of the hoop, and trying to figure out how to best go through the hoop. So as an academic, we're always trained to be able to jump through hoops to raise funding for our labs, and we get our robots to do that.

(Applause)

So another thing the robot can do is it remembers pieces of trajectory that it learns or is pre-programmed. So here, you see the robot combining a motion that builds up momentum, and then changes its orientation and then recovers. So it has to do this because this gap in the window is only slightly larger than the width of the robot. So just like a diver stands on a springboard and then jumps off it to gain momentum, and then does this pirouette, this two and a half somersault through and then gracefully recovers, this robot is basically doing that. So it knows how to combine little bits and pieces of trajectories to do these fairly difficult tasks.

Part 2

So I want to change gears. So one of the disadvantages of these small robots is its size. And I told you earlier that we may want to employ lots and lots of robots to overcome the limitations of size. So one difficulty is: How do you coordinate lots of these robots? And so here, we looked to nature. So I want to show you a clip of Aphaenogaster desert ants, in Professor Stephen Pratt's lab, carrying an object. So this is actually a piece of fig. Actually, you take any object coated with fig juice, and the ants will carry them back to the nest. So these ants don't have any central coordinator. They sense their neighbors. There's no explicit communication. But because they sense their neighbors and because they sense the object, they have implicit coordination across the group.

So this is the kind of coordination we want our robots to have. So when we have a robot which is surrounded by neighbors—and let's look at robot I and robot J—what we want the robots to do, is to monitor the separation between them, as they fly in formation.

[...] So what I want to show you next is a video of 20 of these little robots, flying in formation. They're monitoring their neighbors' positions. They're maintaining formation. The formations can change. They can be planar formations, they can be three-dimensional formations. As you can see here, they collapse from a three-dimensional formation into planar formation. And to fly through obstacles, they can adapt the formations on the fly. So again, these robots come really close together. As you can see in this figure-eight flight, they come within inches of each other. And despite the aerodynamic interactions with these propeller blades, they're able to maintain stable flight.

(Applause)

So once you know how to fly in formation, you can actually pick up objects cooperatively. So this just shows that we can double, triple, quadruple the robots' strength, by just getting them to team with neighbors.

Part 3

So all these experiments you've seen thus far, all these demonstrations, have been done with the help of motion-capture systems. So what happens when you leave your lab, and you go outside into the real world? And what if there's no GPS? So this robot is actually equipped with a camera, and a laser rangefinder, laser scanner. And it uses these sensors to build a map of the environment. What that map consists of are features—like doorways, windows, people, furniture—and it then figures out where its position is, with respect to the features. So there is no global coordinate system. The coordinate system is defined based on the robot, where it is and what it's looking at. And it navigates with respect to those features.

So I want to show you a clip of algorithms developed by Frank Shen and Professor Nathan Michael, that shows this robot entering a building for the very first time, and creating this map on the fly. So the robot then figures out what the features are, it builds the map, it figures out where it is with respect to the features, and then estimates its position 100 times a second, allowing us to use the control algorithms that I described to you earlier. So this robot is actually being commanded remotely by Frank, but the robot can also figure out where to go on its own. So suppose I were to send this into a building, and I had no idea what this building looked like. I can ask this robot to go in, create a map, and then come back and tell me what the building looks like. So here, the robot is not only solving the problem of how to go from point A to point B in this map, but it's figuring out what the best point B is at every time. So essentially it knows where to go

to look for places that have the least information, and that's how it populates this map.

So I want to leave you with one last application. And there are many applications of this technology. I'm a professor, and we're passionate about education. Robots like this can really change the way we do K–12 education. But we're in Southern California, close to Los Angeles, so I have to conclude with something focused on entertainment. I want to conclude with a music video. I want to introduce the creators, Alex and Daniel, who created this video.

(Applause)

So before I play this video, I want to tell you that they created it in the last three days, after getting a call from Chris. And the robots that play in the video are completely autonomous. You will see nine robots play six different instruments. And of course, it's made exclusively for TED 2012. Let's watch.

(Sound of air escaping from valve)

(Music)

(Whirring sound)

(Music)

(Applause) (Cheers)

Unit 10 Julian Treasure: Five ways to listen better

Part 1

We are losing our listening. We spend roughly 60 percent of our communication time listening, but we're not very good at it. We retain just 25 percent of what we hear. Now not you, not this talk, but that is generally true. Let's define listening as making meaning from sound. It's a mental process, and it's a process of extraction.

We use some pretty cool techniques to do this. One of them is pattern recognition. (Crowd Noise) So in a cocktail party like this, if I say, "David, Sara, pay attention," some of you just sat up. We recognize patterns to distinguish noise from signal, and especially our name. Differencing is another technique we use. If I left this pink noise on for more than a couple of minutes, you would literally cease to hear it. We listen to differences, we discount sounds that remain the same.

And then there is a whole range of filters. These filters take us from all sound down to what we pay attention to. Most people are entirely unconscious of these filters. But they actually create our reality in a way, because they tell us what we're paying attention to right now. Give you one example of that: Intention is very important in sound, in listening. When I married my wife, I promised her that I would listen to her every day as if for the first time. Now that's something I fall short of on a daily basis. (Laughter) But it's a great intention to have in a relationship.

Part 2

But that's not all. Sound places us in space and in time. If you close your eyes right now in this room, you're aware of the size of the room from the reverberation and the bouncing of the sound off the surfaces. And you're aware of how many people are around you because of the micro-noises you're receiving. And sound places us in time as well, because sound always has time embedded in it. In fact, I would suggest that our listening is the main way that we experience the flow of time from past to future. So, "Sonority is time and meaning" — a great quote.

I said at the beginning, we're losing our listening. Why did I say that? Well, there are a lot of reasons for this. First of all, we invented ways of recording — first writing, then audio recording and now video recording as well. The premium on accurate and careful listening has simply disappeared. Secondly, the world is now so noisy, (Noise) with this cacophony going on visually and auditorily, it's just hard to listen; it's tiring to listen. Many people take refuge in headphones, but they turn big, public spaces like this, shared soundscapes, into millions of tiny, little personal sound bubbles. In this scenario, nobody's listening to anybody.

We're becoming impatient. We don't want oratory anymore, we want sound bites. And the art of conversation is being replaced — dangerously, I think — by personal broadcasting. I don't know how much listening there is in this conversation, which is sadly very common, especially in the U.K. We're becoming desensitized. Our media have to scream at us with these kinds of headlines in order to get our attention. And that means it's harder for us to pay attention to the quiet, the subtle, the understated.

This is a serious problem that we're losing our listening. This is not trivial. Because listening is our access to understanding. Conscious listening always creates understanding. And only without conscious listening can these things happen — a world where we don't listen to each other at all, is a very scary place indeed. So I'd like to share with you, […] tools you can take away with you, to improve your own conscious listening. Would you like that?

(Audience: Yes.) Good.

Part 3

The first one is silence. Just three minutes a day of silence is a wonderful exercise to reset your ears and to recalibrate so that you can hear the quiet again. If you can't get absolute silence, go for quiet, that's absolutely fine.

Second, I call this the mixer. (Noise) So even if you're in a noisy environment like this — and we all spend a lot of time in places like this — listen in the coffee bar to how many channels of sound can I hear? How many individual channels in that mix am I listening to? You can do it in a beautiful place as well, like in a lake. How many birds am I hearing? Where are they? Where are those ripples? It's a great exercise for improving the quality of your listening.

Third, this exercise I call savoring, and this is a beautiful exercise. It's about enjoying mundane sounds. This, for example, is my tumble dryer. (Dryer) It's a waltz. One, two, three. One, two, three. One, two, three. I love it. Or just try this one on for size. (Coffee grinder) Wow! So mundane sounds can be really interesting if you pay attention. I call that the hidden choir. It's around us all the time.

[…] And finally, an acronym. You can use this in listening, in communication. If you're in any one of those roles — and I think that probably is everybody who's listening to this talk — the acronym is RASA, which is the Sanskrit word for juice or essence. And RASA stands for Receive, which means pay attention to the person; Appreciate, making little noises like "hmm," "oh," "OK"; Summarize, the word "so" is very important in communication; and Ask, ask questions afterwards.

[…] So I invite you to connect with me, connect with each other, take this mission out and let's get listening taught in schools, and transform the world in one generation to a conscious listening world — a world of connection, a world of understanding, and a world of peace.

Thank you for listening to me today.

(Applause)

Unit 11 Gavin Pretor-Pinney: Cloudy with a chance of joy

Part 1

Clouds. Have you ever noticed how much people moan about them? They get a bad rap. If you think about it, the English language has written into it negative associations towards the clouds. Someone who's down or depressed, they're under a cloud. And when there's bad news in store, there's a cloud on the horizon. I saw an article the other day. It was about problems with computer processing over the Internet. "A cloud over the cloud," was the headline. It seems like they're everyone's default doom-and-gloom metaphor. But I think they're beautiful, don't you? It's just that their beauty is missed because they're so omnipresent, so, I don't know, commonplace, that people don't notice them. They don't notice the beauty, but they don't even notice the clouds unless they get in the way of the sun. And so people think of clouds as things that get in the way. They think of them as the annoying, frustrating obstructions, and then they rush off and do some blue-sky thinking. (Laughter) But most people, when you stop to ask them, will admit to harboring a strange sort of fondness for clouds. It's like a nostalgic fondness, and they make them think of their youth. Who here can't remember thinking, well, looking and finding shapes in the clouds when they were kids? You know, when you were masters of daydreaming? Aristophanes, the ancient Greek playwright, he described the clouds as the patron goddesses of idle fellows two and a half thousand years ago, and you can see what he means. It's just that these days, us adults seem reluctant to allow ourselves the indulgence of just allowing our imaginations to drift along in the breeze, and I think that's a pity. I think we should perhaps do a bit more of it. I think we should be a bit more willing, perhaps, to look at the beautiful sight of the sunlight bursting out from behind the clouds and go, "Wait a minute, that's two cats dancing the salsa!" (Laughter) (Applause) Or seeing the big, white, puffy one up there over the shopping center looks like the Abominable Snowman going to rob a bank. (Laughter)

[…] Perhaps you're having a moment of existential angst. You know, you're thinking about your own mortality. And there, on the horizon, it's the Grim Reaper. (Laughter)

[…] But one thing I do know is this: The bad press that clouds get is totally unfair. I think we should stand up for them, which is why, a few years ago, I started the Cloud Appreciation Society. Tens of thousands of members now in almost 100 countries around the world. And all these photographs that I'm showing, they were sent in by members. And the society exists to remind people of this: Clouds are not something to moan about. Far from it. They are, in fact, the most diverse, evocative, poetic aspect of nature. I think, if you live with your head in the clouds every now and then, it helps you keep your feet on the ground. And I want to show you why, with the help of some of my favorite types of clouds.

Part 2

Let's start with this one. It's the cirrus cloud, named after the Latin for a lock of hair. It's composed entirely of ice crystals cascading from the upper reaches of the troposphere, and as these ice crystals fall, they pass through different layers with different winds and they speed up and slow down, giving the cloud these brush-stroked appearances, these brush-stroke forms known as fall streaks. And these winds up there can be very, very fierce. They can be 200 miles an hour, 300 miles an hour. These clouds are bombing along, but from all the way down here, they appear to be moving gracefully, slowly, like most clouds. And so to

tune into the clouds is to slow down, to calm down. It's like a bit of everyday meditation.

Those are common clouds. What about rarer ones, like the lenticularis, the UFO-shaped lenticularis cloud? These clouds form in the region of mountains. When the wind passes, rises to pass over the mountain, it can take on a wave-like path in the lee of the peak, with these clouds hovering at the crest of these invisible standing waves of air, these flying saucer-like forms, and some of the early black-and-white UFO photos are in fact lenticularis clouds. It's true.

A little rarer are the fallstreak holes. All right? This is when a layer is made up of very, very cold water droplets, and in one region they start to freeze, and this freezing sets off a chain reaction which spreads outwards with the ice crystals cascading and falling down below, giving the appearance of jellyfish tendrils down below.

Rarer still, the Kelvin–Helmholtz cloud. Not a very snappy name. Needs a rebrand. This looks like a series of breaking waves, and it's caused by shearing winds—the wind above the cloud layer and below the cloud layer differ significantly, and in the middle, in between, you get this undulating of the air, and if the difference in those speeds is just right, the tops of the undulations curl over in these beautiful breaking wave-like vortices.

All right. Those are rarer clouds than the cirrus, but they're not that rare. If you look up, and you pay attention to the sky, you'll see them sooner or later, maybe not quite as dramatic as these, but you'll see them. And you'll see them around where you live. Clouds are the most egalitarian of nature's displays, because we all have a good, fantastic view of the sky. And these clouds, these rarer clouds, remind us that the exotic can be found in the everyday. Nothing is more nourishing, more stimulating to an active, inquiring mind than being surprised, being amazed. It's why we're all here at TED, right? But you don't need to rush off away from the familiar, across the world to be surprised. You just need to step outside, pay attention to what's so commonplace, so everyday, so mundane that everybody else misses it.

One cloud that people rarely miss is this one: the cumulonimbus storm cloud. It's what produces thunder and lightning and hail. These clouds spread out at the top in this enormous anvil fashion stretching 10 miles up into the atmosphere. They are an expression of the majestic architecture of our atmosphere. But from down below, they are the embodiment of the powerful, elemental force and power that drives our atmosphere. To be there is to be connected in the driving rain and the hail, to feel connected to our atmosphere. It's to be reminded that we are creatures that inhabit this ocean of air. We don't live beneath the sky. We live within it. And that connection, that visceral connection to our atmosphere feels to me like an antidote. It's an antidote to the growing tendency we have to feel that we can really ever experience life by watching it on a computer screen, you know, when we're in a wi-fi zone.

Part 3

But the one cloud that best expresses why cloudspotting is more valuable today than ever is this one, the cumulus cloud. Right? It forms on a sunny day. If you close your eyes and think of a cloud, it's probably one of these that comes to mind. All those cloud shapes at the beginning, those were cumulus clouds. The sharp, crisp outlines of this formation make it the best one for finding shapes in. And it reminds us of the aimless nature of cloudspotting, what an aimless activity it is. You're not going to change the world by lying on your back and gazing up at the sky, are you? It's pointless. It's a pointless activity, which is precisely why it's so important. The digital world conspires to make us feel eternally busy, perpetually busy. You know, when you're not dealing with the traditional pressures of earning a living and putting food on the table, raising a family, writing thank you letters, you have to now contend with answering a mountain of unanswered emails, updating a Facebook page, feeding your Twitter feed. And cloudspotting legitimizes doing nothing. (Laughter) And sometimes we need—(Applause) Sometimes we need excuses to do nothing. We need to be reminded by these patron goddesses of idle fellows that slowing down and being in the present, not thinking about what you've got to do and what you should have done, but just being here, letting your imagination lift from the everyday concerns down here and just being in the present, it's good for you, and it's good for the way you feel. It's good for your ideas. It's good for your creativity. It's good for your soul. So keep looking up, marvel at the ephemeral beauty, and always remember to live life with your head in the clouds. Thank you very much. (Applause)

Unit 12 Margaret Heffernan: Dare to disagree

Part 1

So for 25 years, Alice Stewart had a very big fight on her hands. So, how did she know that she was right? Well, she had a fantastic model for thinking. She worked with a statistician named George Kneale, and George was pretty much everything that Alice wasn't. So, Alice was very outgoing and sociable, and George was a recluse. Alice was very warm, very empathetic with her patients. George frankly preferred numbers to people. But he said this fantastic thing about their

working relationship. He said, "My job is to prove Dr. Stewart wrong." He actively sought disconfirmation. Different ways of looking at her models, at her statistics, different ways of crunching the data in order to disprove her. He saw his job as creating conflict around her theories. Because it was only by not being able to prove that she was wrong, that George could give Alice the confidence she needed to know that she was right.

It's a fantastic model of collaboration—thinking partners who aren't echo chambers. I wonder how many of us have, or dare to have, such collaborators. Alice and George were very good at conflict. They saw it as thinking.

Part 2

So what does that kind of constructive conflict require? Well, first of all, it requires that we find people who are very different from ourselves. That means we have to resist the neurobiological drive, which means that we really prefer people mostly like ourselves, and it means we have to seek out people with different backgrounds, different disciplines, different ways of thinking and different experience, and find ways to engage with them. That requires a lot of patience and a lot of energy.

[…] So it's one thing to do that in a one-to-one relationship. But it strikes me that the biggest problems we face, many of the biggest disasters that we've experienced, mostly haven't come from individuals, they've come from organizations, some of them bigger than countries, many of them capable of affecting hundreds, thousands, even millions of lives. So how do organizations think? Well, for the most part, they don't. And that isn't because they don't want to, it's really because they can't. And they can't because the people inside of them are too afraid of conflict.

In surveys of European and American executives, fully 85 percent of them acknowledged that they had issues or concerns at work that they were afraid to raise. Afraid of the conflict that that would provoke, afraid to get embroiled in arguments that they did not know how to manage, and felt that they were bound to lose. Eighty-five percent is a really big number. It means that organizations mostly can't do what George and Alice so triumphantly did. They can't think together. And it means that people like many of us, who have run organizations, and gone out of our way to try to find the very best people we can, mostly fail to get the best out of them.

Part 3

So how do we develop the skills that we need? Because it does take skill and practice, too. If we aren't going to be afraid of conflict, we have to see it as thinking, and then we have to get really good at it. So, recently, I worked with an executive named Joe, and Joe worked for a medical device company. And

Joe was very worried about the device that he was working on. He thought that it was too complicated and he thought that its complexity created margins of error that could really hurt people. He was afraid of doing damage to the patients he was trying to help. But when he looked around his organization, nobody else seemed to be at all worried. So, he didn't really want to say anything. After all, maybe they knew something he didn't. Maybe he'd look stupid. But he kept worrying about it, and he worried about it so much that he got to the point where he thought the only thing he could do was leave a job he loved.

In the end, Joe and I found a way for him to raise his concerns. And what happened then is what almost always happens in this situation. It turned out everybody had exactly the same questions and doubts. So now Joe had allies. They could think together. And yes, there was a lot of conflict and debate and argument, but that allowed everyone around the table to be creative, to solve the problem, and to change the device.

Joe was what a lot of people might think of as a whistleblower, except that like almost all whistleblowers, he wasn't a crank at all, he was passionately devoted to the organization and the higher purposes that that organization served. But he had been so afraid of conflict, until finally he became more afraid of the silence. And when he dared to speak, he discovered much more inside himself and much more give in the system than he had ever imagined. And his colleagues don't think of him as a crank. They think of him as a leader.

So, how do we have these conversations more easily and more often? Well, the University of Delft requires that its Ph.D. students have to submit five statements that they're prepared to defend. It doesn't really matter what the statements are about, what matters is that the candidates are willing and able to stand up to authority. I think it's a fantastic system, but I think leaving it to Ph.D. candidates is far too few people, and way too late in life. I think we need to be teaching these skills to kids and adults at every stage of their development, if we want to have thinking organizations and a thinking society.

Grammar Summary

UNIT 1: Gerunds and infinitives

When I'm stressed, I enjoy watching movies.
Would you consider having a stressful job?
She recommends getting a pet if you're feeling stressed.

We intend to go for a run later.
Lara hopes to avoid stressful situations.
Do you prefer to exercise in a gym or outdoors?

They love flying / to fly, even though it's stressful.
I hate getting / to get jet lag.

His uncle persuaded him to become a pilot.
The professor reminded us to study for the test.

- Gerunds always follow certain verbs such as *avoid*, *enjoy*, *consider*, *finish*, *imagine*, *recommend*, and *suggest*.

- Infinitives always follow certain verbs such as *decide*, *expect*, *hope*, *intend*, *need*, *plan*, *prefer*, and *want*.

- Both gerunds and infinitives follow some verbs such as *begin*, *continue*, *like*, *love*, and *hate*.

- Infinitives always follow certain verbs when they are combined with objects. These verbs include *allow*, *ask*, *invite*, *encourage*, *expect*, *persuade*, *remind*, and *want*.

UNIT 2: Relative clauses

Captain America is a character who inspires many children.
People (that) our children look up to should be good role models.

Sports heroes, who aren't always examples of good behavior, have a lot of influence over children.
The movie, which is based on the book, was a big success.

The people watching the movie were moved by its positive message.
The hero chosen by most students as their favorite was Katniss Everdeen from *The Hunger Games*.

- We form relative clauses with the relative pronouns *who*, *that*, *which*, *whose*, *where*, and *when*. The relative pronouns *who* (for people) and *that* (for people or things) can be both subjects and objects in sentences.
- Relative clauses give information about the noun that precedes it in the sentence.
- A relative clause is defining if it is necessary for the sentence to make sense.

- A relative clause is non-defining if it gives information that is not essential for understanding the sentence. We use commas at the beginning and end of non-defining relative clauses. We use *which*, and not *that*, in non-defining relative clauses that refer to things.

- Reduced relative clauses do not include a relative pronoun. We form reduced relative clauses by replacing the relative pronouns with an *-ing* or past participle form of the verb.

UNIT 3: Present perfect and present perfect progressive

The world's population has doubled since 1960. Prices have risen, so people are spending less money.	We use the present perfect to describe: • a completed action that has an effect on the present • a past action that continues up to the present • a past action where the specific time is not stated, and we want to emphasize the action
The price of oil has been falling slowly over the past few years. People have been using more oil in the past 20 years.	We use the present perfect progressive to describe: • an activity that started in the past and may or may not be in progress in the present • a recent activity when we want to emphasize the process or duration of the activity • We don't use the present perfect progressive with stative verbs (know, belong, seem, believe, etc.).

UNIT 4: Modals of deduction and speculation

She must be very rich because she lives in a huge apartment in Manhattan. That might not be his real name. She may or may not know that she's broken the law.	• We use must/mustn't, might/might not, may/may not, could/couldn't, and can't (but not can) with the base form of the verb to guess what might be true or correct now.
That might have been Denise who waved at us. She could have given you a fake name. She couldn't have written this note because this isn't her handwriting.	• We use must, might, may, could, and couldn't with have + the past participle to guess what might be true or correct in the past.

UNIT 5: Past perfect and past perfect progressive

She was surprised to get such a good grade on the test because she hadn't studied for it.	• We form the past perfect with *had* (*'d*) + the past participle. • We use the past perfect to talk about an event or action that happened before another event in the past. • We often use the past perfect simple and the simple past together.
He was happy when the bus finally arrived because he had been waiting for three hours.	• We form the past perfect progressive with *had* (*'d*) *been* + *-ing* verb. • We use the past perfect progressive to talk about an ongoing process, event, or action that happened before another event in the past. • We often use the past perfect progressive and the simple past together.

UNIT 6: Phrasal verbs

Are you going to turn down the job offer? They think their new car design will really take off. A lot of people look up to Dr. Takashi. I gave back the money. I gave the money back. She grew up in Singapore. ~~She grew in Singapore up.~~	• We tend to use phrasal verbs in less formal English. • Phrasal verbs are formed with a verb + particle (a preposition or adverb). • Some phrasal verbs can be separated, but some cannot.

UNIT 7: Modals of probability

Robots will work in hospitals in the future. Thanks to new medical technologies, people won't get sick as often.	• We use *will* + verb to describe a future event that is very certain.
People should live much longer in the future. Space tourism is likely to become popular some day.	• We use *should* or *likely to* + verb to describe a future event that is somewhat certain.
Nanoparticles could deliver vaccines one day. In the future, scientists might grow organs in labs.	• We use *may*, *might*, or *could* + verb to describe a future event that is less certain.

UNIT 8: Future perfect and future perfect progressive

Ana will have gotten married by the time she turns 30. I won't have paid off my student loans by 2025.	• We form the future perfect with *will have* + the past participle. • We use the future perfect to describe actions that will be completed by a specific time in the future.
James will have been teaching for more than a year by the time he leaves for Asia. When I finish this course, I'll have been learning Spanish for six years.	• We form the future perfect progressive with *will have been* + the present participle. • We use the future perfect progressive to show that something will continue up until a particular event or time in the future.

UNIT 9: First conditional and second conditional

If the tests are successful, ride-share companies will start using driverless cars.	The first conditional follows the following pattern:
You won't necessarily save money on insurance if you buy a driverless car.	• *if* + simple present, ... *will* + verb
	We use the first conditional to talk about:
	• something that is likely to happen in the future
	• possible situations that are generally true
If you had enough money, which car would you buy?	The second conditional follows the following pattern:
If drivers were less distracted, there would be fewer accidents on the road.	• *if* + simple past, ... *would* + verb
	We use the second conditional to talk about:
	• something that is the opposite of a real situation
	• something that is unlikely to happen in the future

UNIT 10: Reported speech

Kate: "I listen to music on the way to work."
Kate said (that) she listened / listens to music on the way to work.

Sara: "I didn't listen to the lecture."
Sara said (that) she hadn't listened / didn't listen to the lecture.

Jon: "I'm listening to my friend's story."
Jon said (that) he was listening to his friend's story.

Professor: "I was explaining the importance of effective listening."
The professor said (that) she had been explaining the importance of effective listening.

Ava: "I might go to Bali next month."
Ava said (that) she might go to Bali the following month.

Ken: "I'll talk to my parents. I hope they'll listen."
Ken said (that) he would talk to his parents and (that) he hoped they would listen.

Becky: "Did you enjoy the presentation, Alex?"
Becky asked Alex if / whether he had enjoyed the presentation.

Mark: "What type of listening skills have you been studying?"
Mark asked what type of listening skills I had been studying.

The presenter told the audience to think about the last time they felt stressed out.

He warned me that the stove was still hot.

She suggested that I attend a mediation course.

The doctor recommended drinking tea instead of coffee in the morning.

They promised to have dinner together soon.

According to Richard Branson, successful entrepreneurs need to be good listeners.

- We use reported speech to report someone's words or thoughts.
- The most common reporting verb for statements is *say*. After the reporting verb, *that* is optional.

Verb tenses change when we report other people's words:

- Simple present becomes simple past. When the situation is still true at the moment of reporting, the simple present doesn't need to change.
- Simple past usually becomes past perfect, though it may stay as simple past.
- Present progressive becomes past progressive.
- Past progressive becomes past perfect progressive.
- The modal verbs *might*, *should*, *would*, and *could* don't usually change. *Will* becomes *would*. *Must* becomes *had to*.

- The most common reporting verb for questions is *ask*. We don't use *that* after the reporting verb: we refer to the person the question was directed to.

There are other reporting verbs that give more information about the speaker's intention. Common verbs are *tell*, *suggest*, and *promise*. These verbs use other patterns:

- verb + object + *(not)* + infinitive
- verb + object + *that*
- verb + *that*
- verb + *-ing*
- verb + *(not)* + infinitive

- We use *according to* when we want to report a fact as described by somebody.

Pronoun, adjective, and adverb changes

Direct speech	Reported speech	Direct speech	Reported speech
I	he/she	this office	that office
we	they	now	then
my	his/her	today	that day
our	their	tomorrow	the next day
here	there	yesterday	the day before
these	those	last night	the night before

UNIT 11: Articles and quantifiers

I bought a new dress yesterday.
Cloudspotting is an activity I really enjoy.
I find it relaxing to take a walk in a park.

I took photos of clouds and later tried to identify the clouds on the website.
The moon is very bright tonight.
I love looking at the photos of clouds that people send me.

Being surrounded by nature has benefits.
Spending time outdoors can increase happiness.

A report on multitasking is released each / every month.

I receive a large number of emails every day.
There are a few important ways you can reduce stress.

The brain uses a small amount of energy each time we switch tasks.
These days, most people don't have a lot of time to enjoy nature.

We use the articles *a* and *an* before:

• something we mentioned the first time
• something that is one of many

We use the article *the* before:

• something we have already mentioned
• something that is unique
• something that is specific in the given context

We use no article before:

• plural things or people in general
• an uncountable thing in general

• We use the quantifiers *each* and *every* before singular countable nouns.

• We use the quantifiers *a large/small number of* and *a few* before plural countable nouns. They indicate approximate numbers.

• We use the quantifiers *a large/small amount of*, *a lot of*, and *a little (bit of)* before uncountable nouns. They indicate approximate quantity.

If he had known about the issue, he would have told the media.

If they had told us about the problem, we could have fixed it earlier.

She might have stood up to her boss if she had been more confident.

If the whistleblower hadn't leaked the information, we wouldn't know about the corruption.

If I didn't have a smartphone, I probably wouldn't have uploaded the information for everyone to see.

The third conditional follows the following pattern:

- *if* + past perfect, ... *would have* + past participle

- We can use the modals *could (not)*, *might (not)*, *should (not)*, and *must (not)* instead of *would* with *have* + past participle.
- We use the third conditional to talk about something in the past that did not happen. We imagine the event and we imagine the result in the past.

There are two types of mixed conditional sentences:

- *if* + past perfect, ... *would* + verb
- *if* + simple past, ... *would have* + past participle

We use mixed conditionals to talk about:

- an unreal past event and its probable result in the present
- an unreal present situation and its imagined past result

Acknowledgements

The Author and Publisher would like to thank the following teaching professionals for their valuable input during the development of this series:

Coleeta Paradise Abdullah, Certified Training Center; **Tara Amelia Arntsen**, Northern State University; **Estela Campos**; **Federica Castro**, Pontificia Universidad Católica Madre y Maestra; **Amy Cook**, Bowling Green State University; **Carrie Cheng**, School of Continuing and Professional Studies, the University of Hong Kong; **Mei-ho Chiu**, Soochow University; **Anthony Sean D'Amico**, SDH Institute; **Wilder Yesid Escobar Almeciga**, Universidad El Bosque; **Rosa E. Vasquez Fernandez**, English for International Communication; **Touria Ghaffari**, The Beekman School; **Rosario Giraldez**, Alianza Cultural Uruguay Estados Unidos; **William Haselton**, NC State University; **Yu Huichun**, Macau University of Science and Technology; **Michelle Kim**, TOPIA Education; **Jay Klaphake**, Kyoto University of Foreign Studies; **Kazuteru Kuramoto**, Keio Senior High School; **Michael McCollister**, Feng Chia University; **Jennifer Meldrum**, EC English Language Centers; **Holly Milkowart**, Johnson County Community College; **Nicholas Millward**, Australian Centre for Education; **Stella Maris Palavecino**, Buenos Aires English House; **Youngsun Park**, YBM; **Adam Parmentier**, Mingdao High School; **Jennie Popp**, Universidad Andrés Bello; **Terri Rapoport**, ELS Educational Services; **Erich Rose**, Auburn University; **Yoko Sakurai**, Aichi University; **Mark D. Sheehan**, Hannan University; **DongJin Shin**, Hankuk University of Foreign Studies; **Shizuka Tabara**, Kobe University; **Jeffrey Taschner**, AUA Language Center; **Hadrien Tournier**, Berlitz Corporation; **Rosa Vasquez**, JFK Institute; **Jindarat De Vleeschauwer**, Chiang Mai University; **Tamami Wada**, Chubu University; **Colin Walker**, Myongii University; **Elizabeth Yoon**, Hanyang University; **Keiko Yoshida**, Konan University

And special thanks to: **Trudi Edginton, Mamta Nagaraja, Linda Steinbock, Erin Wong, Nadia Ruiz, Shree Bose, Michael Hanley, Laurence Steinberg, Robert Wood, David Walker, Carl Honoré, Mary Kadera**

Credits

Photo Credits

Cover © Yash Mulgaonkar, **3** Michael Hanson/Aurora Photos, **4** (tl) © Dian Lofton/TED, (tr) © TED, (cl) © Robert Leslie/TED, (cr) © James Duncan Davidson/TED, (bl) Mark Fredesjed R. Cristino/Pacific Press/LightRocket/Getty Images, (br) © Ryan Lash/TED, **5** (tl) © Ryan Lash/TED, (tr) © James Duncan Davidson/TED, (cl) © James Duncan Davidson/TED, (cr) © TED, (bl) (br) © James Duncan Davidson/TED, **6** (tl1) Atta Kenare/AFP/Getty Images, (tl2) Keith Bedford/Reuters, (cl1) Rebecca Conway/AFP/Getty Images, (cl2) Dima Korotayev/Stringer/Getty Images News/Getty Images, (bl1) John Moore/Getty Images News/Getty Images, (bl2) Sankei/Contributor/Getty Images, **8** (tl1) Mark Thiessen/National Geographic Creative, (tl2) Enigma/Alamy Stock Photo, (cl1) Tomohiro Ohsumi/Bloomberg/Getty Images, (cl2) Hero Images/Getty Images, (bl1) Giuseppe Cacace/AFP/Getty Images, (bl2) Stan Honda/AFP/Getty Images, **10–11** © Dian Lofton/TED, **12** © Michael Brands/TED, **13** © Dian Lofton/TED, **14** Atta Kenare/AFP/Getty Images, **15** © Trudi Edginton, **17** Steve Debenport/E+/Getty Images, **18–19** VCG/Stringer/Getty Images News/Getty Images, **21** © Dian Lofton/TED, **23** © Dian Lofton/TED, **24** (tl) Dear Blue/Moment Select/Getty Images, (tr) Dimitri Otis/Taxi/Getty Images, (cl) Arek_Malang/Shutterstock.com, (cr) FashionStock.com/Shutterstock.com, **25** © TED, **26** Keith Bedford/Reuters, **27** NASA, **29** Kevin Winter/Getty Images Entertainment/Getty Images, **30–31** AP Images/Kenny Kemp/The Charleston Gazette, **33** © TED, **35** Well Go/Courtesy Everett Collection, **36** Karwai Tang/Contributor/WireImage/Getty Images, **37** © Robert Leslie/TED, **38** Rebecca Conway/AFP/Getty Images, **39** © Linda Steinbock, **41** © Krochet Kids, **42–43** Lars Ruecker/Moment/Getty Images, **45** (t) © Robert Leslie/TED, **46** (c) © TED, **47** © Robert Leslie/TED, **48** Alexander Spatari/Moment/Getty Images, **49** © Cengage Learning, **51** © James Duncan Davidson/TED, **52** Dima Korotayev/Stringer/Getty Images News/Getty Images, **53** © Erin Wong, **55** Time Life Pictures/The Life Picture Collection/Getty Images, **57** Robert Madden/National Geographic Creative, **59** © James Duncan Davidson/TED, **60** (tl) (tr) © TED, **61** © James Duncan Davidson/TED, **62** STR/AFP/Getty Images, **63** Mark Fredesjed R. Cristino/Pacific Press/LightRocket/Getty Images, **64** John Moore/Staff/Getty Images News/Getty Images, **65** © Nadia Ruiz, **67** © Marla Aufmuth/TED, **69** Michael Kirby Smith/The New York Times/Redux Pictures, **71** © TED, **73** Richard Levine/Alamy Stock Photo, **74** John van Hasselt - Corbis/Corbis Historical/Getty Images, **75** © Ryan Lash/TED, **76** Sankei/Contributor/Getty Images, **77** © Shree Bose, **79** Blazic27/iStock/Getty Images Plus/Getty Images, **81** Handout/Getty Images Entertainment/Getty Images, **83** © Ryan Lash/TED, **85** Sean Gallup/Getty Images News/Getty Images, **86** Courtesy of Hippo Water Roller Project www.hipporoller.org, **87** © Cengage Learning, **89** © Ryan Lash/TED, **90** Mark Thiessen/National Geographic Creative, **91** © Michael Hanley, **94–95** Jeff Pachoud/AFP/Getty Images, **97** © Ryan Lash/TED, **98** © TED, **99** © Ryan Lash/TED, **100** Getty Images/Handout/Getty Images News/Getty Images, **101** © James Duncan Davidson/TED, **102** Enigma/Alamy Stock Photo, **103** © Axel Griesch, **105** Josh Reynolds/The Washington Post/Getty Images, **106–107** © Iva Zimova/Panos, **109** © James Duncan Davidson/TED, **111** © James Duncan Davidson/TED, **112** (tl) Jekaterina Nikitina/Stone/Getty Images, (cl) Portra Images/DigitalVision/Getty Images, (bl) Jetta Productions/Iconica/Getty Images, **113** © James Duncan Davidson/TED, **114** Tomohiro Ohsumi/Bloomberg/Getty Images, **115** Rebecca Drobis/National Geographic Creative, **117** Tolga Akmen/Anadolu Agency/Getty Images, **118–119** Blend Images/Alamy Stock Photo, **121** © James Duncan Davidson/TED, **123** Paul Souders/The Image Bank/Getty Images, **124** The Asahi Shimbun/Getty Images, **125** © Cengage Learning, **127** © TED, **128** Hero Images/Getty Images, **129** Courtesy David Walker, **132–133** Richard Nowitz/National Geographic Creative, **135** © TED, **137** © TED, **139** © James Duncan Davidson/TED, **140** Giuseppe Cacace/AFP/Getty Images, **141** © Carl Honoré, **143** © Earl Miller, **144–145** Michael Hanson/Aurora Photos, **147** © James Duncan Davidson/TED, **148** (tl) (tr) (cl) (cr) © TED, **149** © James Duncan Davidson/TED, **150** Roger de la Harpe/Gallo Images/Getty Images, **151** © James Duncan Davidson/TED, **152** Stan Honda/AFP/Getty Images, **153** Bettmann/Getty Images, **155** North Wind Picture Archives/Alamy Stock Photo, **156–157** AP Images/Axel Heimken/Picture-Alliance/dpa, **159** © James Duncan Davidson/TED, **161** © James Duncan Davidson/TED, **162** vm/E+/Getty Images, **163** © Cengage Learning, **166** (t) Greir/Shutterstock.com, (b) © Kem McNair

Illustration & Infographic Credits

16, 28, 40, 54, 66, 78, 92, 104, 116, 130, 142, 154 emc design; **20, 22, 45** (b)**, 46** (t)**, 48, 56, 93, 122, 131, 165** MPS North America LLC.

Data sources for infographics: **16** www.careercast.com, **28** www.apa.org, articles.chicagotribune.com, Annenberg Public Policy Center, University of Pennsylvania, **40** money.cnn.com, **48, 165** www.youtube.com, **54** www.techweez.com, www.dailymail.co.uk, www.medicaldaily.com, **66** en.wikipedia.org, www.livescience.com, www.sapienplus.com, **78** www.moneysmart.gov.au, **92** www.popularmechanics.com, profitable-practice.softwareadvice.com, **104** www.entrepreneur.com, **116** www.nbins.com, **130** transforminc.com, www.getinfrontcommunications.com, **142** www.inc.com, edition.cnn.com, **154** en.wikipedia.org, www.spacesafetymagazine.com, www.mprnews.org

Text Credits

94–95 Sources of data: "3-D Printer": ngm.nationalgeographic.com, December 2014, "What, Exactly, Is a 3-D Printer?": news.nationalgeographic.com, May 2013, **118–119** Sources of data: "Unmanned Flight: The Drones Come Home": ngm.nationalgeographic.com, March 2013, "Drones Soar As Energy's Inspector Gadget At Pipelines, Windmills": news.nationalgeographic.com, September 2015, "5 Surprising Drone Uses (Besides Amazon Delivery)": news.nationalgeographic.com, December 2013, **144–145** Adapted from "This Is Your Brain on Nature": ngm.nationalgeographic.com, January 2016